ATHLETE AND ACTIVIST

ATHLETE AND ACTIVIST

28 SPORTS STARS WHO CHANGED THE GAME

JULES BOYKOFF, ALEX C. DAVIS, AND AMIRA ROSE DAVIS

ILLUSTRATIONS BY MARTIN FRENCH

UNIVERSITY OF ILLINOIS PRESS
Urbana, Chicago, and Springfield

Manufactured in the United States of America
C 5 4 3 2 1
∞ This book is printed on acid-free paper.

Cataloging data available from the Library of Congress

LCCN 2026020079
ISBN 978-0-252-05991-9 (cloth : alk.)
ISBN 978-0-252-04933-0 (ebook)

Publication was supported by a grant from the Howard D. and Marjorie L. Brooks Fund for Progressive Thought.

The manufacturer's authorized representative in the EU for product safety is Mare Nostrum Group B.V., Mauritskade 21D, 1091 GC Amsterdam, The Netherlands. Email: gpsr@mare-nostrum.co.uk

CONTENTS

INTRODUCTION

When Angel City FC took the pitch for its National Women's Soccer League match against the North Carolina Courage in the summer of 2025, players donned T-shirts emblazoned with the phrase "Immigrant City Football Club" across the front. The back of the T-shirt read "Los Angeles is for everyone" and "Los Ángeles es para todos." The action on the field took place after an intense day of protests on the streets of LA where activists stood against violent apprehensions carried out by Immigration and Customs Enforcement and stood up for a city that welcomes immigrants as a vital part of the social fabric. Protests in the streets made space for athletes to take action.

Sports captivate us with their drama and energy, both on and off the field of play. They showcase human effort at its peak: athletes pushing their limits, competing with passion, and achieving feats that seem impossible. These moments of triumph unite us, drawing cheers from stadiums and living rooms alike. Yet, beyond the glory of competition, sports offer a reflection of society itself. They reveal not only our shared values but also the challenges we face. The playing field can highlight teamwork and perseverance, but it can also expose barriers of race, gender, class, sexuality, and power.

Athletes stand at the intersection of performance and public life. Their skill inspires millions, making them symbols of excellence and dedication. At the same time, their visibility places them in a unique position to address issues that extend far beyond their sports. When they speak out, they seize opportunities to amplify critical messages. But they also step into a space fraught with criticism and risk.

The tension between their role as competitors and their potential as changemakers shapes their impact on and off the field.

Few moments capture this duality more powerfully than the 1968 Olympic medal ceremony in Mexico City, where United States track and field athletes Tommie Smith and John Carlos raised their black-gloved fists in silent protest. Standing atop the podium, their message was clear and unforgettable: the fight for racial justice and human rights could not wait. Their gesture, though silent, spoke volumes to a watching world. It also came with steep consequences. They were expelled from the Olympic Village, vilified by the media, and faced threats to their safety and careers. Yet their courage became a symbol of hope and a rallying cry for generations to come. Decades later, President Barack Obama would reflect on their actions, acknowledging that their protest "woke folks up and created greater opportunity for those that followed." The stance that Smith and Carlos took on sport's biggest stage is arguably the most iconic, symbolically powerful example of athlete activism in action. But what is athlete activism exactly? One gaggle of scholars recently defined athlete activism as "direct action to bring about change to a social or political issue," distinguishing it from athlete advocacy, which they described as "communicating and working on behalf of those affected by issues in society." Scholar Joseph Cooper drills deeper, offering specific tenets of athlete activism and advocacy. He writes that athlete activism involves intentionally moving beyond individual activity and toward collective action alongside like-minded others in ways that are oppositional and disruptive. Athlete activists arrive with concrete demands for change and are linked to social movements. Athlete advocacy, on the other hand, consists of actions designed to generate awareness of injustice, to provoke public introspection, and to support political causes.

Athlete activism tends to veer toward direct engagement with politics through in-your-face action, while athlete advocacy tends to take the subtler form of symbolic actions that ripple with political import but are not necessarily deliberate political undertakings. An athlete can also be a quiet advocate by example. Some of the athletes featured in this book are known less for their direct political actions than for what they represent socially. Let's be clear: representation absolutely matters. Being the first athlete to achieve a sporting milestone can inspire us even when they are not outspoken about politics. The actions of these barrier breakers can nevertheless stand as powerful symbols of political possibility. And they can till the political soil for other forms of athlete action.

To be sure, activist, advocate, and barrier breaker are not wrought-iron categories. Native American athlete Jim Thorpe excelled at the 1912 Olympics, a forerunner who embodied Indigenous excellence. Later he spoke out as an activist about "Pretendians" in Hollywood—white actors playing Native roles. Serena Williams served as a role model for modern-day African Americans by dominating the tennis circuit and only later in her career became outspoken about racism ingrained in the sport. Even the example that kicked off this book—Angel City FC's on-field stance in support of immigrants—rides the line between taking intentional, oppositional action that is both collective and disruptive and implicitly advocating for more humane policing.

One thing's for sure: Smith and Carlos's principled stand wasn't an outlier. Throughout history, athletes have found ways to make their voices heard. Some have taken public stands, like Muhammad Ali refusing to serve in the Vietnam War or Billie Jean King demanding equal pay and respect for women in tennis. Others have broken barriers simply by succeeding in environments where they weren't welcome, like trailblazers Jackie Robinson, who joined Major League Baseball in 1947, or Althea Gibson, who broke the color line in tennis *and* women's golf. Whether through protest or perseverance, athletes have used their platforms to challenge the status quo and inspire change.

The courage to speak out isn't without cost. LeBron James, one of the most celebrated athletes of his generation, has experienced this firsthand. After his home was vandalized with a racial slur, James spoke out about the persistence of racism, saying, "No matter how far you come, there are always people who want to let you know that you are still beneath them." His words resonated deeply with many, but his criticisms of President Donald Trump drew backlash, including the infamous remark by a television host who told him to "shut up and dribble." These moments reveal the stark divide between the admiration athletes receive for their talents and the resistance they face when their messages challenge societal norms.

Political pundits flung flak at LeBron James, but the basketball star benefited from the presence of an ascendant Black Lives Matter movement. Vibrant activist movements can help shield outspoken athletes, blunting criticism from the opposition. In other words, social *movements* scythe space for athlete-activist *moments*.

Dr. Harry Edwards—a prime mover in the Olympic Project for Human Rights of the late 1960s, the group of athlete activists that included Tommie Smith and John Carlos—credits the Black Lives Matter movement for helping to spur what he calls the fourth wave of athlete activism, which includes LeBron James and many athletes featured in this book. This follows the first wave that was grounded in the era of racial segregation, the second wave nestled in the folds of the Cold War and jump-started by an emergent civil rights movement, and the third wave inspired by the Black Power movement of the 1960s and 1970s. Edwards points to social media technology as key to propelling tech-savvy athletes to command a bigger stage and one that they can control. Social media have afforded athletes a direct path to becoming athlete activists through digital populism. On the flip side, they also enable trolls of the ugliest order to spread their often-anonymous vitriol at these forthright athlete activists.

The response to athletic activism, and indeed the athletes themselves, often reveals larger ideas about who belongs in sports and on what conditions. Following the 2020 Olympic Games in Tokyo, World Athletics found that 87 percent of all online abuse toward athletes was aimed at women, with 63 percent of all the abuse targeting Black women. The fight for access and investment in women's sports has always been a political fight. Similar to the way the civil rights movement and Black Lives Matter created space for athletic activism, women's liberation and #MeToo cleaved space for athletes to address gender discrimination in sport and beyond. These overlapping waves and undercurrents expand our understanding of athletic activism. The athletes in this book demonstrate how vast and varied those waves can be and include stories from undercurrents below the surface that can easily go overlooked.

The idea that political movements foster athlete-activist moments also undergirds journalist Howard Bryant's conception of "the Heritage," a tradition of athlete activism passed down through the generations of Black athletes, from Paul Robeson to Serena Williams. African American athlete activists are featured prominently in this book. As scholar Amy Bass notes, "The black athlete serves as one of *the most visible integrated* racial subjects in modern society, seen in all facets of media, cheered by millions of fans, teamed with white counterparts, and, at least on the surface, accepted." For African American athletes, so much is at stake. Scholar Louis Moore writes, "For the black community, sports represented tangible proof that democracy would triumph over discrimination, and equally important, sports offered proof that whites would accept black people." Black athletes are both a monument to meritocracy and a lightning rod for racist heat.

The athletes featured in this book have navigated significant challenges with determination and vision. Some, like Megan Rapinoe and Colin Kaepernick, have become modern icons of activism. Others, like Chris Mosier and Bilqis Abdul-Qaadir, have fought battles for representation and inclusion that resonate deeply but may not be as widely known. Together, their stories form a tapestry of courage, resilience, and the relentless pursuit of justice.

Selecting which athletes to include was itself a process of reflection and conversation. The book's contributors debated, discussed, and deliberated, guided by the idea that meaning emerges through dialogue. We couldn't include everyone and had to make some tough exclusions: formidable athletes who used their platforms to drive toward the horizon of justice like Brittney Griner, Jim Brown, Simone Biles, Craig Hodges, Layshia Clarendon, Curt Flood, Rosalie Fish, William Henry Lewis, Joe Louis, Billy Mills, Renée Richards. We invite readers to engage in their own reflections. Who deserves recognition in the history of athlete activism? Which voices resonate with your values? How do these stories connect to the struggles and triumphs of today?

To convey the span of shifting cultural and political terrain that athletes have traversed—and the evolving pressures and possibilities that have shaped their engagement—we have organized the profiles in this book not by chronology alone, but through four thematic categories that reflect both the emphases of their times and the broader toolkit from which athlete activists can draw. "Reveal" celebrates barrier breakers whose courageous presence casts a spotlight upon hypocritical, exclusionary systems. "Resist" features protesters who used their hard-won platforms for direct dissent. "Reframe" recognizes visionaries who labored to redefine what power, voice, and visibility can mean in sport. And "Reimagine" highlights innovators who have taken up the mantle of activists who came before them, expanding the field to include concern rooted in identity, care, faith, and culture. While these categories represent the prevailing strategies of respective eras, they are not hard boundaries. Many, if not most, of the athletes included here move fluidly across them, reminding us that athlete activism is as dynamic and evolving as the contexts to which it responds.

We believe that the inclusion of art—Martin French's vivid illustrations—is vital to this project. Art can help us see the world afresh. It can reset our mindset. It can carve space to meditate on the imaginable. Art, like the actions of the athletes in this book, is grounded in politics. It can, in special moments, "relate to the popular struggles of the day," as critic Ben Davis writes, and contribute "decisively to our images of the struggles of which they were a part." We urge readers to slow down and meditate on each illustration. How does the art that accompanies each written entry move us beyond words toward a deeper sense of comprehension?

Sports offer us more than entertainment; they reveal what's possible. They show us moments of extraordinary human achievement but also serve as a stage for justice, resilience, and transformation. The athletes in this book didn't just compete to win—they sought to change the game itself, opening doors for others and challenging society to be better. Their actions remind us that courage isn't confined to a single arena and that each of us has the capacity to make a difference.

Athlete activism is a response to overlapping systems of injustice. In this book we celebrate athlete activists who have courageously elbowed their way into the political conversation, thereby widening the public imagination. As you read, think about the risks these athletes took and the legacies they left behind. Consider how their stories inspire your own sense of possibility. Sports are a mirror of who we are, but they can also be a vision of who we could become. Let these athletes show you what it means to rise to a challenge and to leave a mark that reaches far beyond the scoreboard.

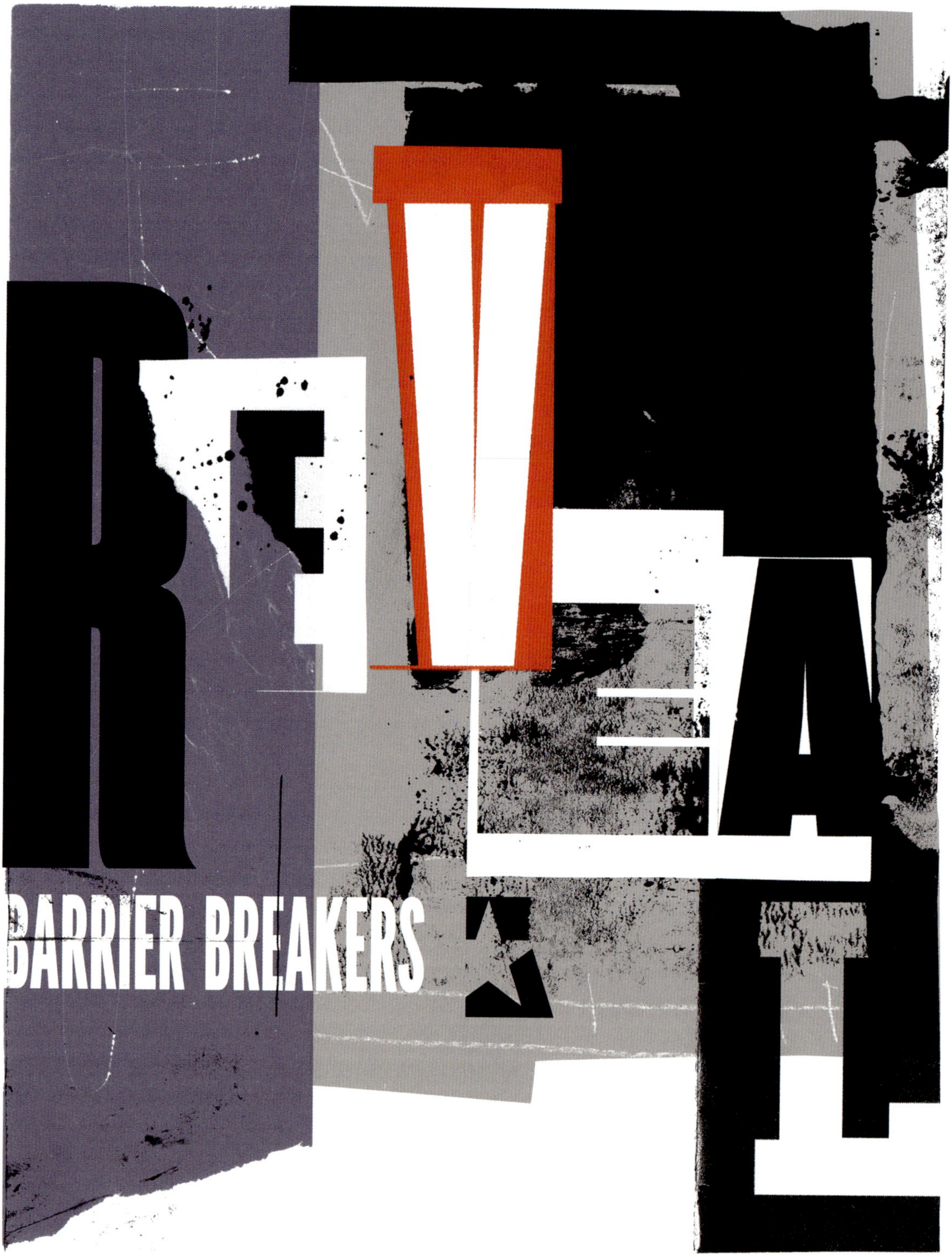
BARRIER BREAKERS

REVEAL

Barrier breakers exposed the boundaries and silences within sport; through their presence, they forced hidden structures into view.

JIM THORPE
FRENCH

JIM THORPE

Growing up in the Oklahoma Territory, Jim Thorpe did not saunter through life with a pocket full of silver spoons. Born to a father of Sac and Fox and Irish descent and a mother who was Potawatomie with Menominee, Kickapoo, and French ancestry, Thorpe learned the meaning of hard work at a young age. While his family wasn't poor, they lived a hardscrabble existence, working the land for food and fun, with Jim and his brother Charlie responsible for small-game hunting for meat. As journalist Sally Jenkins put it, "A breakfast of champions for Thorpe was no bowl of cereal. It was fried squirrel with creamed gravy after running all night in the woods at the heels of his dogs."

The General Allotment Act of 1887, also known as the Dawes Act, passed in the year Thorpe was born, and it lived up to Theodore Roosevelt's assessment as "a mighty pulverizing agent to break up the tribal mass." The Act parceled out land to Native Americans to be held in trust by the federal government for twenty-five years. After that, legal title would be granted to Native landholders. "Extra" land not held by tribal members was sold back to the government, which then sold it to white settlers at a profit. The Dawes Act shattered the traditional rhythms of Native communities, including those of the Thorpes. The Interior Department overseeing the process outlawed Native traditions, including feasts, and encouraged Indians to cut their hair, cease speaking Native languages, and, in short, assimilate to white, Western ideals.

Thorpe's parents valued education. After attending the Haskell Institute, an Indian boarding school in Kansas, Jim Thorpe eventually made his way to the Carlisle Indian Industrial School, a government-operated education facility in Pennsylvania, where he was a student from 1904 to 1913. Toward the end of his dazzling, multi-sport athletic career at Carlisle, he traveled to Stockholm for the 1912 Olympics where he pulled the rare double-feat of winning gold in both the decathlon and the pentathlon. For the former he was awarded a silver Viking ship courtesy of the Russian tsar, and for the latter King Gustav V of Sweden gave him a bronze bust. These trophies were prominently displayed during Thorpe's victory tour in the United States, which took place not only at the Carlisle Indian Industrial School, where "a raucous battalion of students" celebrated as "a team of boys pulled a carriage carrying Thorpe," according to his biographer David Maraniss, but also in places like New York and Philadelphia.

Based on his dominance at the 1912 Games, the ABC television program "Wide World of Sports" designated him the "Greatest Athlete of the Century." This echoed Sweden's King Gustav V who famously told Thorpe, "Sir, you are the greatest athlete in the world." *The New York Times* anointed Thorpe—whom they once dubbed "the Redskin from Carlisle"—as the "finest all-around athlete in the world." Thorpe kindled pride in Native Americans and non-Natives alike. Due to Thorpe and his classmate, Hopi runner Lewis Tewanima, who won silver in the 10,000-meter run in Stockholm, Carlisle Indian Industrial School provided more points to the US tally than any other educational organization. Ironically, American Indians would not be recognized as US citizens until the passage of the Indian Citizenship Act in 1924.

But Thorpe's triumph was short-lived. In the wake of the Stockholm Games, the International Olympic Committee stripped him of his medals for breaking the amateur code. In 1909–1910 he had received a small sum of money—$60 a month—for playing semiprofessional baseball. Although, as his biographer Kate Buford points out, "He had made less in one season of baseball than a white collegian could make from writing one newspaper article," the IOC showed no mercy and commandeered his medals and trophies.

After a journeyman's career as a professional athlete, Thorpe went on to become an actor in Hollywood where he protested "Pretendians" who impersonated Native Americans and snapped up the precious few Native roles that existed. He assisted activist groups like the War Paint Club, a collection of Native actors in Hollywood who pushed back against Indigenous stereotypes in film and the practice of "redfacing," or feigning to be Native. The group also demanded more lucrative contracts for Native actors. As Maraniss notes, in Hollywood, Thorpe "grew as a leader, fighting for fair treatment for his people, doggedly looking after his rights and those of hundreds of other Indians trying to eke out livings in an industry where they were considered superfluous."

Despite the shine of Hollywood, Thorpe wasn't exactly raking in steady pay. In 1932, he lacked the cash to attend the Olympic Games in Los Angeles and the Los Angeles Organizing Committee failed to offer him free tickets. It was only the intervention of US Vice President Charles Curtis—a Native American of Kaw descent—that led to Thorpe getting a pass to attend the Games. Around this time, Thorpe increasingly turned to alcohol to cope with his hardships. In October 1944 he was arrested for driving under the influence.

Meanwhile, a campaign had emerged to get Thorpe's medals restored, with people like Major League Baseball's Branch Rickey and US Senator Mike Monroney of Oklahoma lending their support. Prominent sports journalist Grantland Rice led the charge, writing in 1949 to Avery Brundage, who was then vice president of the International Olympic Committee, "It would, of course, be wonderful for old Jim if he could get those trophies back that he lost at Stockholm. I have talked with him and he seems to be more interested in that than anything else." Brundage, who had also participated in the 1912 Olympics where he was tromped by Thorpe in the decathlon and pentathlon, was unmoved. He wrote back, "I doubt if the men who received Thorpe's medals would give them up." Noting that the medals were handed out by the Swedish Organizing Committee, he stated, "I am very doubtful that they would have any interest in the subject."

Brundage, Thorpe's self-appointed nemesis, was notorious for his racist, sexist, and classist views. Plus, Brundage was wrong. Some Olympic bigwigs *did* take an interest. In 1982, at the behest of United States Olympic Committee President William Simon, the IOC voted to return Thorpe's gold medals. In a ceremony in early 1983, IOC President Juan Antonio Samaranch presented Thorpe's children with replacement gold medals as well as replica silver medals for each of them. It was not until 2022 that the IOC finally restored his records and medals into the organization's official history. In 2024, US President Joseph Biden posthumously awarded Thorpe the Presidential Medal of Freedom, the highest civilian honor in the United States.

Of course, Thorpe was not there to enjoy this himself. He died of a heart attack in 1953 in poverty and under the spell of alcohol. He was living in a trailer park in Lomita, California, near Long Beach. But his legend lives on.

JACKIE ROBINSON
Dodgers
FRENCH

JACKIE ROBINSON

On April 15, 1947, Jack Roosevelt Robinson took the field as a player for the Brooklyn Dodgers. Before that day, modern Major League Baseball had been strictly segregated. After that day, professional baseball—and American sports in general—would begin a transformation toward reflecting the fullness of the nation's diversity and talent. It is now an annual tradition, for example, that on April 15, every Major League Baseball player wears a jersey emblazoned with Robinson's number 42. No matter their skin tone or nationality, players stand united to honor the legacy that brought them together. But that legacy of unifying transformation was never guaranteed success. It required the courage, tenacity, integrity, and athletic genius of many—spearheaded by Jackie Robinson. As Cornel West put it, "more even than Abraham Lincoln and the Civil War, or Martin Luther King, Jr. and the Civil Rights movement, Jackie Robinson graphically symbolized and personified the challenge to the vicious legacy and ideology of white supremacy in America."

Robinson was born on January 31, 1919, in Cairo, Georgia, to a family of sharecroppers. A year later, after Robinson's father left, his mother took the children to Pasadena, California. She raised them there as a single parent among extended family. Despite the prejudice the Robinsons faced living in relative poverty as the only Black family in an affluent white area, several of the children excelled. Robinson's older brother, Matthew (or "Mack"), won silver behind Jesse Owens in Berlin's 1936 Olympic Games. And Jackie Robinson established himself as an all-around sports star, first at John Muir High School, then at Pasadena Junior College, and finally at UCLA, where he became the first student to letter in varsity football, basketball, baseball, and track.

After leaving UCLA just shy of graduation in 1941 due to financial hardship, Robinson pursued several occupations in sports. He started as an athletic director for a short-lived government youth program. But when the program ended, he moved to Honolulu where he played semi-professional football as a running back until the United States entered World War II—and Robinson entered the Army.

By 1944, Robinson had reached the rank of lieutenant and was leading a platoon of the 761st Tank Battalion stationed in Fort Hood, Texas. There, while on a military bus, Robinson refused a bus driver's order that he move to the back of a bus. He knew Army regulation, and it prohibited such discrimination. By the end of the bus ride, however, he was taken into custody and brought before a captain. This officer, as Robinson put it, asked him "real, nice, objective questions like, 'Don't you know you've got no right to be sitting up there in the white part of the bus?'" When Robinson stood up for his rights, the captain only became increasingly angry and defensive. "As serious as the situation was," recalled Robinson, "I had to laugh . . . I was up against one of those white supremacy characters. Everything would have been all right if I had been a 'yassuh boss' type."

Far from being all right, because of the bus incident Robinson not only missed deployment with his outfit but also found himself facing court-martial in a system that did not typically offer defendants good odds. Fortunately, he had a competent attorney and motivated allies. His lawyer was able to confound the cadre of false witnesses that testified against him. In addition, several of his fellow Black officers wrote to the press. They were able to bring enough national attention to the proceedings that an unjust verdict would have created a scandal the Army did not want. In the end, Robinson was acquitted and given an honorable discharge. Now out of the Army, not because of bullets from Nazis abroad but due to the bigotry of racists at home, he returned to sports and began playing baseball in the Negro Leagues.

During that time, the manager of the Brooklyn Dodgers, Branch Rickey, launched an international search for a Black ballplayer who could spearhead the integration of Major League Baseball. Rickey was looking for a player who possessed two characteristics. Obviously, the man would need to be a world-class baseball talent. But more importantly to Rickey's mind, he would need to command exceptional moral tenacity and restraint.

When the Dodgers' extended global search landed on Jackie Robinson, it was something of a surprise. There were players with better statistics, greater fame, more talent. Robinson, moreover, had consistently displayed zero tolerance for racist acts and language. Everything about his past marked him as more of a proud warrior with no patience for injustice rather than a gradualist diplomat. It turned out, however, Rickey was searching for someone who could be both diplomat and warrior. During their famous first meeting, Robinson's combination of passion, pride, personableness, and charismatic presence impressed Rickey enough to sign him on the spot. Both men understood that they were about to launch a powerful cultural attack on Jim Crow. And their aim was not simply to topple the sinister system of segregation in Major League Baseball. They hoped their campaign would root it out of the nation altogether.

But Robinson, Rickey, and the Dodgers were hardly heroic individuals rising up without encouragement and support. Their success built upon years of groundwork laid by activists who saw sports as a pivotal arena in the larger struggle for racial justice. As Peter Dreier observes, "Rickey's plan came after more than a decade of effort by black and left-wing journalists and activists to desegregate the national pastime." Far from launching a bold, original vision to affect the country through baseball, Robinson and Rickey were acting to realize the long-standing campaign of Black and liberal journalists, civil rights activists, America's Communist Party, and many others. Integrate Major League Baseball, the idea went, and the country would soon have to follow.

But soon, of course, is a relative term. In his first years in the league, Robinson became a lightning rod for the expressions of society's prejudice, both on and off the field. Threats, taunts, jeers, insults, snubs—they all came at him with a vengeance. And although Robinson felt it all acutely, he faced it resolutely, helping expose racism's moral and spiritual bankruptcy on the nation's favorite stage. Despite the extra stress and adversity that came with breaking baseball's color barrier, Robinson earned National League Rookie of the Year honors. He went on to lead the league in stolen bases twice. He led the league's second basemen in double plays four times. He was a six-time All-Star, won the batting title and National League MVP in 1949, and led the Dodgers to six World Series with one World Series Championship during his ten-year career.

After baseball, Robinson continued to throw his full weight into the push for justice and equality in America. In his 1972 autobiography, *I Never Had It Made*, Robinson called for the hiring of a Black manager in Major League Baseball, confronting the racist stereotypes that continued to bar qualified Black candidates from leadership roles. He co-founded Freedom National Bank in Harlem, one of the largest

Black-owned banks in the country at the time, as part of his enduring commitment to Black economic empowerment. He also frequently called out politicians—including presidents—for failing to stand for civil rights. Arnold Rampersad recounts, for example, that "Robinson was increasingly harsh on President Eisenhower, who in his travels overseas mouthed 'words of great hope and encouragement concerning freedom and independence' to emerging nations such as India and Afghanistan but preached patience to blacks at home." As Robinson put it, "If there had been vigorous and uncompromising leadership from the White House . . . America would never have had the shame of a Little Rock or a Poplarville." Robinson pursued these justice-minded endeavors and others, not just as a famous baseball player, but as an actor, an author, a newspaper columnist, a philanthropist, a collaborator with Dr. Martin Luther King Jr., and the first Black vice president at a major American corporation. His wide-ranging efforts continued to be marked by the strategy of integration, courage, and nonviolent restraint that characterized his time in the Major Leagues.

For many critics, however, Robinson's strategic choices as an activist were far too gradualist. Malcolm X, to cite a particularly public example, charged Robinson with conniving capitulation to the status quo, accusing him of "still trying to win 'the Big Game' for your White Boss." This excerpt from Robinson's reply is representative: "Whether you like this country or not is of little concern to me. America is not perfect, by a long shot, but I happen to like it here and will do all I can to help make it the kind of place where my children and theirs [whites'] can live in dignity . . . You mouth a big and bitter battle, Malcolm, but it is noticeable that your militancy is mainly expressed in Harlem where it is safe. I have always contended for your right—as for that of every American—to say and think and believe what you choose. I just happen to believe you are supporting and advocating policies which could not possibly interest the masses . . . I will always be happy to associate myself with decent Americans of either race who believe in justice for all."

Jackie Robinson, whatever we might want him to have been, was always his own man and always fighting for every one of us.

Althea
GIBSON
FRENCH

ALTHEA GIBSON

Althea Gibson had many journeys in her lifetime. From the South Carolina fields to the concrete streets of New York as a child. From makeshift Harlem tennis courts to champion of the world at Wimbledon. From reluctant activist to outspoken athlete to immortal trailblazer. In many ways, the memories and celebrations of her life, such as the statue in Flushing Meadows where the US Open takes place, hold her frozen in place. But Gibson's story is one of motion. Her athletic success may be one for the storybooks, but her activism is more than mere footnote.

Gibson was born in rural South Carolina in 1927. Her parents were sharecroppers in the corn and cotton fields who joined the thousands of Black Americans who migrated north and west in search of opportunities and reprieve from the racial terror of the Jim Crow South. Leaving South Carolina for New York when Gibson was only three, her family eventually settled in Harlem, on West 143rd Street, between Lenox and Seventh avenues. In Harlem, Gibson grew up playing a variety of sports, relishing the competition. "Basketball was my favorite," she wrote, "but any kind of ball would do." She also dabbled in handball and even boxing. Tennis, however, became her gateway to the world.

Gibson's aptitude as a tennis player was apparent early on. As a teenager, her potential attracted the attention of many elite Black adults who began to support her development in the sport. This included musician Buddy Walker and schoolteacher Juan Serrell who introduced her to Fred Johnson, a tennis pro at the African American Cosmopolitan Tennis Club, one of the top Black clubs in the country. Soon

Gibson was playing tennis in places populated by the Black upper class, including tennis clubs, Black colleges, and American Tennis Association (ATA) tournaments. The ATA was the response to the lingering segregation of the United States Lawn Tennis Association (USLTA).

Gibson's rise in tennis soon would challenge the color line being maintained by the USLTA. As Gibson began competing against—and beating—white women, the barriers of entry to the upper echelons of white tennis began to crumble. While the USLTA initially tried to prevent Gibson from competing in the prestigious National Lawn Tennis Championship, she would eventually break the color line and become the first Black person to compete in the USLTA championships.

Despite her tennis success, Gibson found trailblazing a lonely, ongoing battle. Part of it had to do with her personality. As she put it in her memoir, "I didn't like people telling me what to do. Take it from me, you can get in a lot of hot water thinking like that." Scholar Jennifer Lansbury noted, "She was extremely competitive and confident, even cocky, and the combination could be difficult to take." In part because of her personality but mostly because of ingrained racism, Gibson was socially ostracized from the white competitors on the tour. The sport of tennis has always been exclusive. A working-class Black girl like Gibson represented a challenge to the lily-white country club sport. Yet Gibson pressed on.

Gibson became the first African American to win a Grand Slam title when, in 1956, she clinched the French Open. This paved the way for further success. Subsequently, she triumphed at Wimbledon and the US Nationals (now the US Open) in 1957 and 1958, solidifying her status as one of the greatest tennis players of her generation.

"Shaking hands with the Queen of England was a long way away from being forced to sit in the colored section of the bus going into downtown Wilmington, North Carolina," Gibson said when reflecting on her journey to the top of tennis. Her success led to many Black sportswriters calling her "the Jackie Robinson of Tennis." However, Gibson was reluctant to take up that mantle. Gibson wrote, "I am a tennis player, not a Negro tennis player. I have never set myself up as a champion of the Negro race." Gibson saw the "great value" of what Robinson did: "If he hadn't paved the way, I probably never would have got my chance." And yet she resisted advocating for civil rights with the same tactics. "I have to do it my way," Gibson wrote.

Gibson was aware that being a barrier breaker in sports was symbolically important and that it was significant to others. She wrote, "I try not to flaunt my success as Negro success. It's all right for others to make a fuss over my role as a trail blazer, and, of course, I realize its importance to others as well as to myself, but I can't do it." Throughout her tennis career, Gibson continued to be a barrier breaker but a reluctant advocate for racial equality. She understood the symbolic value of her successes but remained singularly focused on her game. She remained steadfast in this approach, even when journalists, perhaps especially those in the Black press, wanted her to be an outspoken athlete activist who converted her "tennis achievements into a rousing crusade for racial equality, brass band, seventy-six trombones, and all." But, she explained, "I feel strongly that I can do more good my way than I could by militant crusading. I want my success to speak for itself as an advertisement for my race." In short, at this phase of her career, racial representation was enough.

As her tennis career came to a close, however, Gibson found herself in position to break yet another sporting color line, and this time she was prepared to raise her voice. In 1964, Gibson became the first Black woman to join the LPGA tour, breaking the color line in women's professional golf. According to Gibson's biographer, Ashley Brown, the athlete was emboldened by the rise of the civil rights movement and more willing to speak out about discrimination she faced in golf. In this phase of her life and career, Gibson became the athlete activist that she had resisted during her tennis career. Not only was Gibson more outspoken about racial prejudice, but she also challenged the lack of investment in women's sport, the financial realities of professional tennis and golf, and the continued barriers to participation in both sports. "They call me the queen of the court," Gibson lamented, "but I can't eat a crown."

Gibson continued to write memoirs and narrate her own story about her life. She lived on her terms and wanted to be remembered on her own terms as well. Perhaps she wasn't as outspoken as Jackie Robinson and not as radical as some wanted her to be. But she found her own way to push for change. "I still feel that my life as a Black woman and international golf and tennis player speaks loudly and clearly for my race," Gibson wrote. "I feel that I have set a good example which can be followed by any young people. I have proved that it is the person [who] counts in the long run, regardless of race, creed or color."

Gibson passed away in 2003. Her legacy continues to reverberate across the sports she championed and the society she lived in. In chronicling her life, Ashley Brown aptly asserts that Althea Gibson provokes the question "What do we ask of our cultural heroes?" Indeed, Gibson is a reminder that there is no single course of athletic activism and that the label can be freighted with stressors. We remember Gibson as a tennis trailblazer. That becomes her primary story of activism. Yet her golf career, her memoirs, her life as a singer who put out an album—*Althea Gibson Sings*—and appeared twice on *The Ed Sullivan Show* all offer a fresh lens for understanding Gibson as a change agent. It also reminds us that our understanding of athletic activism should not be static or prescriptive. Gibson and many athletes featured in this book create a capacious rendering of athletic activism that allows us to see the many ways people have used sport to remake this world into a better, more equitable place.

EARLENe
BROWN
FRENCH

EARLENE BROWN

Earlene Brown is hard to capture. She defies categorization. She lived a dozen lives. Brown probably would not have called herself an activist. She was just Earlene, unapologetically and relentlessly herself.

In many ways, Brown's entire life was a constant rebellion. A rebellion against what Black women should look like, what they should act like, where they should work, and certainly what they should say. A paragon of courage, Earlene Brown said whatever she wanted to say. As much as the world attempted to shrink Brown into a respectable, prescribed box, Brown resisted at every turn and gleefully took up space wherever she was. "Most girls played with dolls, paper cut-outs, little toys," Brown said of her childhood in the 1940s. "I was big. I liked to move around, play football, baseball, climb trees, and play hide-and-seek."

Born in Latexo, Texas, in 1935, Earlene Brown had always been athletic. "I was a born Hercules," Brown explained. Her father played semi-pro baseball in the Negro Leagues. Brown credits her strength to him, but her tenacity, resiliency, and wit she got from her mother. At the age of three, Brown moved with her mother to California. Growing up in Los Angeles, Brown had many interests, including volleyball, softball, football, and ballet. As a teenager, however, she started to formally compete in track and field. While Brown began as a sprinter, a teacher soon introduced her to field events. She might have been a latecomer to shot put and discus, but Brown was a quick learner: just three months after making her Amateur Athletic Union (AAU) competitive debut, Brown would hold the national record in both events.

As Brown's star was rising, her home life was crumbling. Brown was married and had a young son, and her husband objected to the attention and opportunity she was gaining. When Brown was tapped for the 1956 Olympics, her husband issued an ultimatum: go to the Olympics or stay married. Brown packed her bags right there and headed off to the first of three Olympic Games in which she would compete.

With no formalized support, Brown funded her own way to the Olympics. She opened a beauty shop and did hair, cleaned houses, hustled people at poker, and dominated local bowling tournaments. Local Black institutions, such as her church and the *Los Angeles Sentinel*, the city's Black newspaper, also held community campaigns to raise money to support her athletic career. Assembling funds to compete in this nontraditional way was certainly cumbersome and challenging. Yet being independently sponsored is one of the reasons Brown was able to become an athlete that the United States Olympic Committee (USOC) could not control, although they tried.

Brown competed in international competitions and state-sponsored "goodwill tours" in the 1950s and 1960s. The State Department's use of athletes, particularly Black athletes, to advance Cold War politics and statecraft politicized every competition Brown entered. She became accustomed to foreign reporters constantly asking about US race relations and just as familiar with the USOC's desire for no one to answer such questions. Brown often used a joking nature in response, employing humor to diffuse tension. After Olympic trials in 1956, Brown admitted it was hard "dealing with white supervisors" and needing to "take backseats to whites on the busses," but then added, "well white girls had to take a backseat when I competed in my athletic events!" When asked about the "race problem" a few years later, Brown replied with a sly smile that she "never ran into it in my life" then added "let me take that lie back," launching into a story about a discriminatory meal experience prior to 1960 Olympics trials.

Her skills and humor as a storyteller meant that Brown was a media darling *and* that the folks who governed US Olympic sports did not, or perhaps could not, police her voice in the way they approached other outspoken athletes. When telling the story about being denied service in Corpus Christi, Brown joked about how shocked her white teammates were and how nasty the food looked anyways. "I couldn't see why they were so prejudiced when they were serving garbage like that," Brown candidly joked. The sportswriters ate it up. They often framed her through descriptions of her size, her body, and her temperament, referring to her as "220 pounds of joy" and a "big bundle of good humor."

Yet as journalist Michael Davis observed, "glib sportswriters . . . failed to understand the depths of the revolution inside her." As Brown headed to Rome for the 1960 Summer Olympics, she was already at odds with members of the US Olympic Committee. The United States government was interested in having their Olympic athletes perform shows of goodwill to the Russian athletes. A tea party was planned, and they made it mandatory for US Olympians to attend. Brown refused.

"When you say Russia and the United States have to go to a tea and that's compulsory to go, to me this is politics," Brown recalled, "I wouldn't go. So, I caused quite a lot of trouble that year because I wouldn't go." Brown was uninterested in being a chess piece in the geopolitical game that the emerging superpowers were playing. She wanted to play, and she wanted to travel, and she wanted to connect with other athletes on her terms, free from the politics of their respective countries. So Earlene Brown set out to do just that.

Brown was the life of the Olympic Village in every Games in which she competed. Because she had paid her own way to the Olympics, the US team administrators had markedly less control over her. Brown wandered around without chaperones, hosted rambunctious poker games, and threw the best dance parties in the Olympic Village. Her parties were so popular that the press covered them with glee and the US Olympic Committee gave up trying to regulate her.

Brown remained uninterested in Cold War politics or the narratives that the State Department hoped to produce using their Black Olympic athletes. She continued to forge her own global friendships that often challenged the official narratives. Most notably, Brown maintained a friendship with the Russian women throwers against whom she competed. Over the course of three Olympics, countless dual meets, and other international competitions, Brown and Russian athletes like Tamara Press and Galina Zybina flaunted their friendship in the face of growing Cold War tensions. On one occasion, Brown picked up her Russian competitors when they were in Los Angeles and spent the entire day driving them around in a convertible, showing them the city and introducing them to her friends and family.

Brown's jovial nature and penchant for parties and poker often belied a clear-headed critique of the geopolitics and Black women athletes' role in it. She was an outspoken advocate for racial and gender justice inside the sphere of sport and outside it too. For Brown, the "story of Negro girls in the Olympics" was a frustrating and unfulfilled fairytale. "They [Negro girls] are all Cinderella girls," Brown told reporters in 1964. "They pulled themselves up beyond where they really were supposed to be. None of them were supposed to be at London, Helsinki, Melbourne,

Rome, or Tokyo; or riding first class on a jet plane, eating a five-course dinner and drinking champagne." Brown knew that the fairytale was short-lived. "They come back home and at 12 o'clock their carriage turns to a pumpkin and they got bills, bills, bills," she concluded. "They are the ones holding up the high standards of American athletics, the ones all America cheers. But how many people realize just how it really is?" Brown openly confronted racism and sexism and was an early advocate for what today people call intersectional analysis: understanding the reverberating multiplier effect of oppression through race, class, gender, and sexuality.

Brown loved the world she got to experience via sports but remained unflinchingly clear about the national and international politics that structured sports and her experience within them. Brown was not an activist who boycotted or demonstrated in traditional ways, but she was an outspoken advocate who was ungovernable. Brown challenged the way the US Olympic Committee and State Department used and disposed of their Black athletes.

After the 1964 Tokyo Olympics, Brown left track and field entirely. She briefly bowled competitively before turning to roller derby. She enjoyed a second career as a famous roller derby star. Brown kept returning to athletic activity because she enjoyed the opportunity to travel and connect with people. "Sports teaches you to have patience and tolerance. It takes away ignorance and gives you survival," Brown explained. "In sports you learn about different people—their attitudes, personalities, the rich and the poor. You get to evaluate your position in the world."

Earlene Brown was an athlete who brought her voice, passion, humor, and wit to everything she did, regardless of the pushback she received or the expectations that others tried to foist upon her. She was outspoken and defiant, but her protests were subtle. She simply refused to comply with unreasonable demands, called things out, and kept moving forward. Brown remains a model for living a life out loud and on your own terms.

RUDOLPH
FRENCH

WILMA RUDOLPH

From the moment of her birth, Wilma Rudolph was already defying expectations. She came weeks early and weighed a mere four and a half pounds. Born in St. Bethlehem, Tennessee, Rudolph was the twentieth of twenty-two children in her family. Her father was a railroad porter and took other jobs as necessary to support the family, while her mother worked as a domestic in the nearby homes of white people. Rudolph's early childhood was largely shaped by sickness. Her bouts of pneumonia, scarlet fever, and polio ultimately left her scrawny, weak, encumbered with leg braces, and unable to walk. Undeterred by her physical disability, Rudolph's mother was determined to see her daughter regain mobility and was fiercely committed to providing her care. Rudolph would say later, "My doctors told me I would never walk again. My mother told me I would. I believed my mother."

As with many places in the segregated and rural South, Clarksville, Tennessee, had no medical institutions for African Americans. Fortunately, Meharry Medical College was located in nearby Nashville. This historically Black medical college and hospital was the preeminent medical institution for African Americans in the country. Because of widespread segregation, Black medical professionals came from all over to study and train at Meharry. Every week Rudolph and her mother would take the hour-long bus ride to Nashville to get treatment. At home, her siblings took turns massaging her legs daily. At twelve years old, after years of treatments and massages, Rudolph removed her leg braces and walked on her own.

Rudolph wasn't walking for long—soon she was running everywhere. She earned the nickname "Skeeter" because she was always buzzing around quickly like a mosquito. Rudolph followed her older sister into the sport of basketball and quickly excelled on the court. She was named a starter from her freshman year at the segregated Burt High School. Her speed on the court caught the eye of a referee named Ed Temple, who was also the track coach of the Tennessee State University Tigerbelles.

Tennessee State, a historically Black college in Nashville, boasted the preeminent women's track program in the country. At a time when most colleges were not investing in competitive athletic programs for women, Black schools in the South stood out for the opportunities they provided for women athletes. Tennessee State offered summer training camps, scholarships, and travel opportunities. When Coach Temple saw Rudolph run up and down the basketball court, he instantly started recruiting her for his program. As a high schooler, Rudolph began to run track with the Tennessee State program. Her early successes landed her a spot on the 4×100-meter relay team heading to the 1956 Olympics in Melbourne. At fifteen years old and just three years removed from wearing her leg braces, Rudolph competed in her first Olympic Games and earned a bronze medal.

Upon returning from the Olympics, Rudolph prepared to finish high school and to officially enroll at Tennessee State. In her senior year, however, she found herself unexpectedly pregnant. Undeterred, Rudolph gave birth to her daughter, graduated high school, and earned a scholarship to run with the Tigerbelles, enrolling at TSU in 1958. Her parents and sister stepped in to help care for her child while she was competing. While at Tennessee State, Rudolph emerged as a dominant talent on an already dominant team. In 1959, she competed in the Pan American Games, earning a silver and gold medal in the 100-meter dash and the 4×100-meter relay, respectively. Rudolph also racked up medals in the Amateur Athletic Union (AAU) championships, winning four consecutive 100-meter titles and three indoor titles. She was a dominant athlete.

As a sophomore, Rudolph and seven of her teammates earned places on the 1960 Olympic team heading to Rome. Once there, Rudolph won a gold medal in the 100-meter and 200-meter competitions as well as the top of the podium in the 4×100-meter relay, becoming the first American woman to win three gold medals in a single Olympics. Her on-the-track success garnered international attention and her "beautiful" and "dainty" appearance off the track led her to be crowned "darling of the Games." The 1960 Olympic Games were the first televised Games, and the increased media attention on Rudolph made her a global sensation. She was invited to the White House—where she and her teammates had a thirty-five-minute meeting with President John F. Kennedy—and featured on game shows and in numerous ads and commercials. Yet, because of amateurism rules, Rudolph was prevented from earning a single cent.

Newspapers from around the world covered the unlikely rise of the "black gazelle" who had survived crippling childhood illness to become the fastest woman in the world. Mainstream presses in the United States applauded "Wonderful Wilma" and the way she "glamorized" track. Meanwhile, Black sports writer Doc Young noted that "long and leggy" Rudolph being nationally and internationally described as beautiful was "indisputable proof that things are improving for the Negro." Despite the global accolades and the American flag draped around her in victory, Rudolph was well aware that she was returning to the Jim Crow South and to a country that was rife with racism.

Back in Clarksville, Tennessee, her hometown planned to welcome her home with a parade. When Rudolph heard that it was going to be segregated, she refused to attend. The town relented and her parade was the first integrated event in Clarksville history. A local white judge spoke at the parade and took the opportunity to demand racial integration. After the parade, military higher-ups at nearby Fort Campbell Army Base welcomed participants of all races, hosting a parachute demonstration and a reception. This would mark the beginning of Rudolph's burgeoning activist influence.

Rudolph was also tapped to go on State Department-sponsored trips abroad as a "Goodwill Ambassador" aimed at advancing Cold War propaganda. However, Rudolph used these trips to connect with Black people across the African diaspora. Her trips to places like Dakar and Ghana helped shape her growing consciousness. Rudolph described feeling "at home" on her trips, noting that she "just went out like I belonged there, and they accepted me." In 1963, three weeks after returning from West Africa, Rudolph led a direct-action protest to desegregate white-owned businesses in Clarksville, including a local diner.

In addition to her travels, Rudolph's post-career experiences made her more critical of American society. Rudolph had spent the first seven years after her retirement in 1962 moving around the country in search of a stable job. Chasing offers to do recreation work or coach athletics, Rudolph bounced to Indiana, and then Maine, and finally Michigan before she ended up moving back to Tennessee after none of the offers lasted very long. Frustrated with the lack of opportunity and still faced with a family to feed, Rudolph became depressed. "I was besieged with money problems,"

Rudolph recalled, "I felt exploited both as a woman and as a black person, and this bothered me very much."

In the 1970s, Rudolph wrote a memoir in hopes of telling her own story in a way that was both inspiring and that allowed her to voice her critiques of society. "Fact of the matter is that black women athletes are on the bottom rung of the ladder," she reflected. "When their track careers are over, no matter what they have accomplished in the Olympics, there is no place for them to go. They wind up drifting back to where they began, and nobody ever hears from them again." Her memoir would continue to elevate her voice. Later it would be adapted for a somewhat sanitized made-for-TV movie, released in 1977, starring a young Denzel Washington and Cicely Tyson. Shirley Jo Finney played Wilma.

Rudolph remained outspoken about racial oppression and gender equality. She became a staunch advocate for women in sports and was a fixture in the track and field world. On the advice of her friend Bill Russell, a fellow Olympian at the 1956 Melbourne Games, she relocated to Los Angeles to get a fresh start. There she dove full-bore into organizing with the Watts Community Action Committee. She continued this on-the-ground community work in Chicago with the Youth Foundation alongside Mayor Richard Daley.

In the summer of 1994, she was diagnosed with aggressive brain cancer. She passed away four months later. She was fifty-four years old.

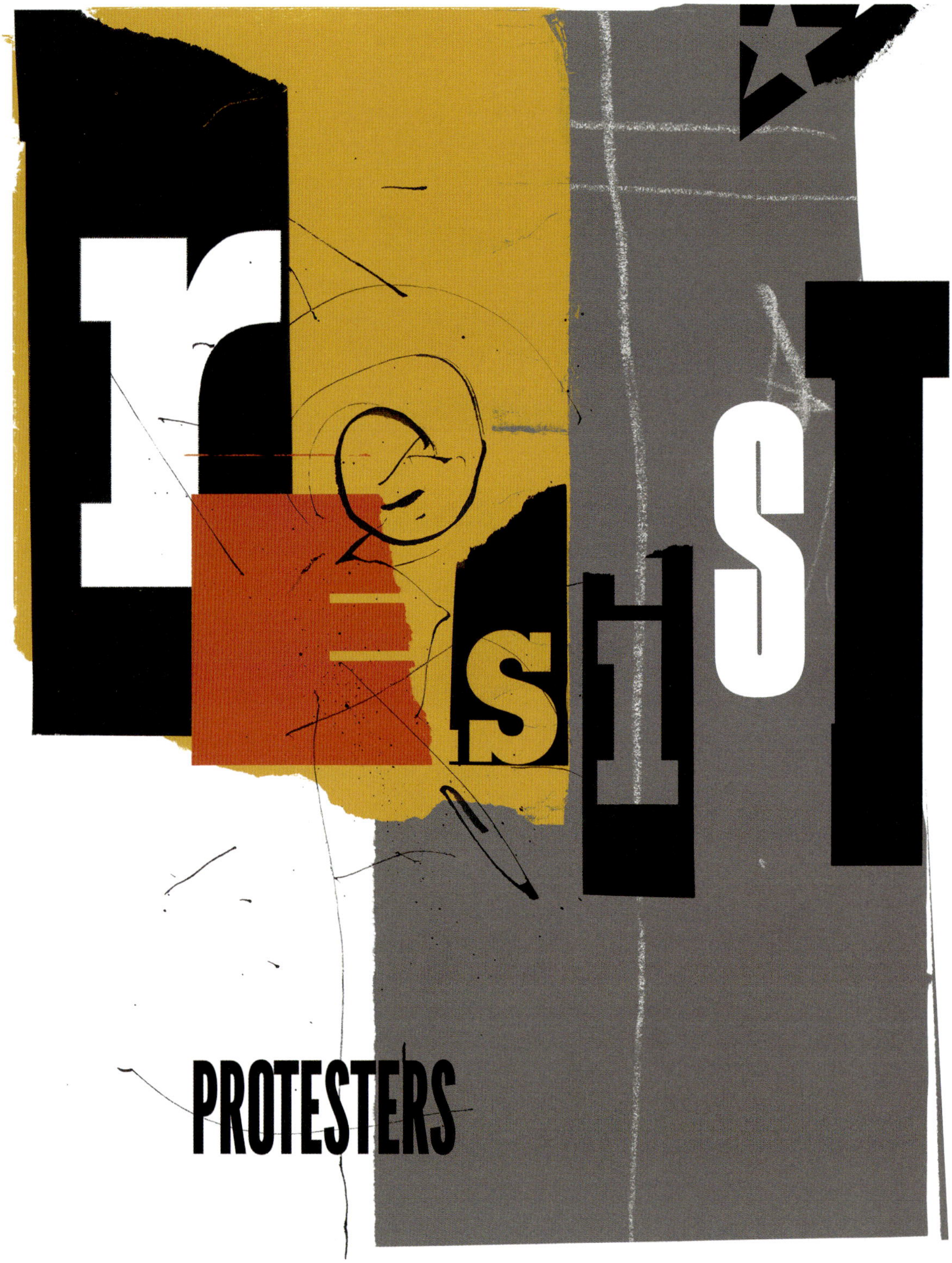
resist
PROTESTERS

RESIST

Protesters refused silence. Through protest, boycott, or withdrawal, they made sport a stage for dissent.

PAUL
ROBESON

PAUL ROBESON

One measure of an athlete activist's power is the ferocity with which the powerful try to squelch their dissent. By that standard, Paul Robeson was one of the most powerful athlete activists of the twentieth century.

Robeson was a jaw-droppingly talented multi-sport athlete who lettered fifteen times in four sports at Rutgers University: football, basketball, baseball, and track and field. At Rutgers, where he was only the third African American student to ever attend, he was an All-American defensive end in football, and eventually he was inducted into the College Football Hall of Fame. Robeson also enjoyed a professional football career with the Akron Pros and the Milwaukee Badgers while simultaneously attending Columbia University Law School, where he earned a law degree. He accomplished all this while experiencing blatant racism: some universities like Washington and Lee and Georgia Tech refused to play against him because he was Black. Robeson described how in one game against West Virginia an opposing player "leaned forward and said, 'Don't you so much as touch me, you black dog, or I'll cut your heart out.'" After smashing the opponent to the turf, Robeson retorted, "I touched you that time. How did you like it?" Teammate Hildrus A. Poindexter described how Robeson was not only a fierce competitor but also a mentor to younger players: "As a lineman I came under the tutelage of Paul Robeson. I worshipped Robeson and absorbed his every principle and tactic for playing on the line."

Robeson's sporty roots were overshadowed by his remarkable career as a singer, actor, and radical political figure who openly espoused socialism. Robeson maintained a firm determination to fight for socialism, or as he put it in his autobiography, "my deep conviction that for all mankind a socialist society represents an advance to a higher stage of life—that it is a form of society which is economically, socially, culturally, and ethically superior to a system based upon production for private profit." Robeson's commitment to the power and righteousness of socialism never wavered.

For his political beliefs, the US government went on an unremitting quest to suppress his dissent, even canceling his passport, which prohibited the highly sought-after performer from traveling around the world to make a living. In August 1950, *The New York Times* reported in a front-page story, "Although neither State Department nor Immigration officials would make extended comment, it was learned that Robeson's activities in left-wing movements and his outspoken criticism of this country's international dealings had much to do with the revocation of the passport."

The newspaper of record in the United States deployed passive voice to describe the situation, but Robeson's response was anything but passive. He denounced President Harry Truman's administration as attempting "to silence the protests of the Negro people." Robeson was a wildly popular performer overseas—from London to Moscow and beyond—so depriving him of travel meant winching shut his income spigot abroad while simultaneously making him a politically radioactive person at home. Robeson finally recovered his passport in 1958, the same year the US Supreme Court ruled that the government could not withhold someone's passport because of their political "beliefs and associations."

Social critic Howard Bryant argues that Robeson poured the foundation for "the Heritage," a lineage of African American athlete activists who rebelled against the white-supremacist worldview that Black people, should they wish to be full democratic citizens, needed to perform the docile role of "Good American." Even though Robeson is better known for his life as an entertainer on the stage, Bryant places him in the pantheon of Black athlete activists who comprise "the Heritage," alongside icons like Muhammad Ali, Serena Williams, John Carlos, and Tommie Smith. Robeson "was the original conscience and soul of the Heritage," writes Bryant. "By risking his enormous fame and wealth to advocate for improving the Black condition, Robeson lost his money but gained his people. When it comes to the Heritage, Robeson was its charter member and first casualty."

One could say that Robeson, whose father had escaped slavery to fight for the Union in the Civil War, had political struggle in his DNA. Robeson wrote, "Let me make one thing very clear: I care nothing—less than nothing—about what the lords of the land, the Big White Folks, think of me and my ideas. For more than ten years they have persecuted me in every way they could—by slander and mob violence, by denying me the right to practice my profession as an artist, by withholding my right to travel abroad. To these, the real Un-Americans, I merely say 'All right—I don't like *you* either!'"

As a singer, he became widely known for his baritone renditions of spirituals. Eventually he emerged as a transnational superstar of the stage whose reprise of *Othello* is rated one of the all-time best by theater critics. He commanded packed concert halls across Europe. Robeson had a preternatural gift for languages and was prone to hunkering down for extensive periods of time with a bundle of books. Languages that he studied and spoke included Spanish, Mandarin, Gaelic, Greek, Latin, Russian, Efik, Hebrew, Swahili, Norwegian, and Portuguese. Robeson biographer Gerald Horne notes that his dexterity with languages brought an added benefit: "When Robeson could speak and sing to the thousands who amassed to hear him in their language, it struck a deep chord, endearing him to those assembled and driving many more to his revolutionary banner."

Upon Robeson's death, Coretta Scott King dubbed him "one of the finest artists, most brilliant minds and greatest champions of human rights that has lived in this century." He had eminent comrades around the world, from future founding father of Ghana Kwame Nkrumah to Indian Prime Minister Jawaharlal Nehru to US Vice President Henry Wallace. Baseball phenom Babe Ruth sent Robeson his best regards on his forty-sixth birthday. Malcolm X was an admirer, as was actor Lena Horne. But Robeson was not content with fame and accolades. He aimed to use his notoriety to improve the lives of people everywhere. He was a radical internationalist who saw class struggle and the fight for racial justice as necessarily transnational. He was an avid supporter and funder of the Council on African Affairs, a group that fought to decolonize the Caribbean and Africa. He petitioned the United Nations to acknowledge genocide against African Americans in the United States. He spoke out against US intervention on the Korean Peninsula.

Robeson also stood firm against red-baiting by the House Un-American Activities Committee (HUAC). The committee's political inquisition was a response to public comments that Robeson made in Paris where he suggested that working-class African Americans would not fight the war against the Soviet Union. However, his comments were twisted by the Associated Press, which misquoted him as saying that the US government resembled Adolf Hitler and his propaganda minister Joseph Goebbels and that the Soviet Union had "raised our people to the full dignity of mankind." This misrepresentation earned him an invitation in 1956 to a HUAC hearing where he was disparaged by pathbreaking baseball star Jackie Robinson.

Even though Robeson had helped smooth the path for Robinson to ascend to Major League Baseball, Robinson did not return the favor when he appeared under the hot congressional spotlight. Although Robinson started his testimony by acknowledging Robeson as "still a famous ex-athlete and a great singer and actor," he eventually pivoted into attack mode: "I know that I've got too much invested for my wife and child and myself in the future of this country, and I and other Americans of many races and faiths have too much invested in our country's welfare, for any of us to throw it away because of a siren song sung in bass." Robinson then stated, "We can win our fight without the Communists and we don't want their help." Members of the Committee were delighted with Robinson's testimony. *The New York Times* piled on, printing Robinson's testimony in full and penning an editorial that discredited Robeson as a Russian puppet: "Mr. Robeson has attached himself to the cause of a country in which all men are equal because they are equally enslaved." Although Robinson later wrote in his autobiography that he regretted falling into the trap of attacking a fellow Black man, the public turmoil was a key factor in the revocation of Robeson's passport the following year.

Political power is often most effective when it is least observable. The US government worked doggedly behind the scenes to undermine Robeson at every turn, maligning him as a Soviet apologist and dupe. A victim of Cold War hysteria, Robeson never swerved off his radical political path. He was not merely an athlete with a conscience, but someone who was enmeshed in movements for radical political change. He was a man of deep, unswerving conviction until the very end. In his poem "Ode to Paul Robeson," Chilean poet Pablo Neruda wrote, "Paul Robeson, / you sang with Lincoln, / covering the sky with your holy voice, / not only for Negroes, for the poor Negroes, but for the poor, / whites, / Indians, / for all peoples."

ROSE
ROBINSON
FRENCH

EROSEANNA "ROSE" ROBINSON

In the waning days of summer in 1959, Chicago was overrun with sporting frenzy. The White Sox were in the American League pennant race for the first time in decades, and over two thousand athletes from twenty-four countries were arriving to compete in the third Pan American Games. From the outset, the Pan Am Games were a bit of a mess. Chicago had been a last-minute location change, and there were a number of logistical issues and mix-ups, including the seventeen members of the Chilean women's basketball team being packed into just two hotel rooms. By the time the pomp and circumstance of the opening ceremonies began, officials hoped the pageantry and sweeping displays of nationalism would distract onlookers from the less savory headlines. As the US national anthem started to play, the crowd in Soldier Field rose to its feet in excitement. But Eroseanna Robinson stayed sitting. The track and field athlete was not there for the bloated displays of American greatness. To her, the anthem and the flag represented war, injustice, and hypocrisy. She would stay in her seat.

Eroseanna Robinson—also called Rose or Sis—was born in 1925 in Chicago. She was the second of three daughters born to Claudius and Mary Robinson. The Robinsons were a lower-middle-class family who lived on the South Side of Chicago. Claudius's job as a mail carrier allowed them to move to Ada Street on the periphery of the Englewood neighborhood, which was starting to see the effects of "white flight": the migration of white people from racially diverse urban areas to more racially homogenous suburbs and exurbs. It also put the Robinson girls in walking distance to Copernicus Playground and Recreational Center. All three of the girls were athletes and very good ones at that. In 1943, Rose, along with her sisters Adrienne and Bernice, led Copernicus to the Central Amateur Athletic Union (AAU) track title. They earned four gold medals and two silvers between them, including in the 4×100-meter relay in which the sisters made up three-quarters of the team. Two years later they would lead the historic Wabash YMCA to a volleyball state title, winning the finals by a score of 69–11. Bernice would go on to compete in the 80-meter hurdles at the 1948 London Olympics.

Rose Robinson's love of athletics was rooted in the fact that they tested her mentally and physically. Sports gave her a sense of focus and drive, bolstering her confidence—all skills that she took with her to her job as a social worker and to her budding involvement in the civil rights movement.

When Robinson moved to Cleveland to work in a community center, she started to get heavily involved with the city's local chapter of the Congress of Racial Equality (CORE). By 1952 she was a leader within the small chapter and led a direct-action protest at a segregated skating rink. Historian Victoria Wolcott writes about the Skateland protest in her book *Race, Riots, and Rollercoasters: The Struggle over Segregated Recreation in America*, in which she details the fact that Robinson led these "skate-ins" over two nights, drawing the bulk of the attention and animosity of the white patrons, and eventually even sustaining a broken arm from their violent reaction. "Rose Robinson's athleticism was always central to her political practices," notes Wolcott. "When she darted around white skaters while attempting to desegregate [Skateland] . . . she demonstrated her athletic skill in the face of an aggressive white mob determined to trip her."

While in Cleveland, Robinson also continued to compete in track and field with Cleveland Recreation. By the time she was back in Chicago in the late 1950s, she had become a very notable high jumper on the AAU circuit. In 1958, Robinson won the high jump at the AAU National Championship and earned a spot on the National Women's Track and Field team. This predominantly Black team was scheduled to go to Russia to compete in a State Department track meet aimed at using Black athletic labor to advance Cold War policy abroad. Immediately after earning a place on the team, Robinson told reporters she was not going to Russia, saying, "I don't want to be used as a Political Pawn."

Robinson's refusal to promote US foreign policy abroad is notable because it came at a time in which the federal government was invested in using Black athletes, musicians, and dancers to attempt to shield the country from the global critiques of Jim Crow practices. Athletes like Jesse Owens, Althea Gibson, and Bill Russell all participated in "goodwill tours" staged by the US Department of State at one time or another. Robinson's very public refusal not only opened the door to public conversations about the propaganda value of these "goodwill tours," but also placed her in the political crosshairs of the State Department.

One year later and just six months after sitting for the anthem at the Pan Am Games, Robinson was arrested on charges of tax evasion over the amount of $386. When brought before the judge, she refused to pay, citing the US government's propensity for violence and war. Robinson said, "If I pay income tax I am participating in that destruction." The judge sentenced her to a year and a day in jail. While in jail, Robinson engaged in a hunger strike, refusing to eat or drink. She became so weak that officials had to carry her in and out of the courtroom. Her hunger strike garnered national attention as hundreds of protesters and letters of support poured in to back the "athlete wasting away in prison."

Later, after her release, Robinson said that her hunger strike was "an endurance test—much like athletics . . . the discipline needs are the same . . . maintenance of form with no wasted motion, detachment from distraction, effort equal to challenge, never leaning towards the finish prematurely, striding evenly and in a balanced way."

In the years after her release, Robinson continued her activism, mostly organizing with a pacifist group called the Peacemakers. She would employ the hunger-strike tactic again when she and Wally and Juanita Nelson were arrested for attempting to eat at a segregated restaurant in Maryland. The trio was participating in the Congress of Racial Equality's targeted desegregation tactics along Route 40, a popular corridor connecting Washington, DC, and Maryland. The Freedom Riders targeted this stretch of highway because it was often traveled by state officials heading to work in the capital.

In 1961, Robinson's arrest, trial, and hunger strike once again garnered national attention. Known as the "Elkton Three," the coverage of Robinson and the Nelsons helped launch increased pressure on segregationist establishments along Route 40. Over the next few months CORE continued to target numerous restaurants along the route. The campaign eventually resulted in the successful desegregation of Route 40. "The discipline and skill that Robinson demonstrated on the track field was invaluable in her political work," notes Victoria Wolcott. "Both took enormous stamina and courage."

Robinson's story has largely been recovered and told through the lens of Colin Kaepernick and his national anthem protests. Yet Robinson's refusal to stand for the anthem is only a small piece of her larger story. Rose Robinson is one of the greatest examples of an athlete activist. She lived her life at the nexus of those two identities and used her athleticism to inform her activism and her athletic platform to highlight her activism. Robinson remained steadfast and courageous, resisting and pushing for social change until her death in 1976. She was only 52 years old.

MUHAMMAD
ALI
FRENCH

MUHAMMAD ALI

Muhammad Ali is one of the most captivating figures in history. Not just sports history, but world history. He underwent a remarkable evolution from Cassius Marcellus Clay, the 1960 Olympic boxing champion, into the radical Black freedom fighter Muhammad Ali and ultimately into the pliable symbol of capitalism who ignited the Olympic cauldron at the 1996 Atlanta Summer Games.

Ali came to fame as a hugely successful boxer with a dazzling personality. He was the first pugilist in history to win the world heavyweight championship three separate times, including in phantasmagoric fashion in 1974 in the "Rumble in the Jungle" against hard-punching George Foreman in Zaire (Democratic Republic of the Congo) where Ali, the unequivocal underdog, miraculously emerged victorious. Ali successfully defended his heavyweight title on nineteen occasions. Wherever Ali went, public attention followed. As Gerald Early noted, "Ali had been a lightning rod for the culture's irrationality all of his life, sometimes provoking it purposely, sometimes a veritable representation of it himself." This athlete activist was complex.

Ali grew up in Louisville, Kentucky, at a time when public spaces were segregated by race. His family was firmly rooted in the working class. His father, Cassius Marcellus Clay Sr., was a painter while his mother, Odessa Grady Clay, labored as a household domestic. In his autobiography, Ali described being denied service at a local restaurant after returning to Louisville with his gold medal from the 1960 Rome Olympics. Rather than the cheeseburger and vanilla shake he ordered, he received a hefty helping of racism. Ali, gold medal draped around his neck, was told "We don't serve Negroes." He left the restaurant, medal in tow, and "lost it on purpose." He wrote, "The world should know the truth—it's somewhere at the bottom of the Ohio River."

Still, Ali's Olympic victory paved a path for public adulation. The clean-cut quipster became famous for his poetic sassafras and quicksilver wit. A 1963 *Time* magazine cover story heaped up the hyperbole: "Cassius Clay is Hercules, struggling through the twelve labors. He is Jason, chasing the Golden Fleece. He is Galahad, Cyrano, D'Artagnan. When he scowls, strong men shudder, and when he smiles, women swoon. The mysteries of the universe are his Tinker Toys. He rattles the thunder and looses the lightning."

Ahead of his time in so many ways, Clay subtly pressed against predominant gender norms, often chirping, "Ain't I beautiful?" Journalists described all this as "showboating tendencies" and "cute vanities," so long as he steered clear of overt politics. Clay was portrayed in *The New York Times* as "boxing's Cicero in resin . . . a fresh breeze in an otherwise becalmed sport," along the way heralding "his love of boxing and country." Angling for a championship bout, Clay told the journalist, "I'm just the heavyweight champion that the world needs. We need a man with personality, color, patience, charm, who'll talk to all reporters—give 'em just what they want. A man who's willing to cooperate in every way."

Ali's relationship with the public and press U-turned in 1964 when Ali ceased to "give 'em just what they want." After winning the heavyweight boxing title from the heavily favored Sonny Liston, Clay flinted a political firestorm when he announced he had joined the Nation of Islam, the group headed by Elijah Muhammad that aimed to create a separate society for its members rather than adopting the integrationist approach of the civil rights movement. In doing so, Clay showed he was no longer "willing to cooperate in every way." After he first took the name Cassius X, Elijah Muhammad bestowed upon him the noble name Muhammad Ali. His name change symbolized not only Black pride but also a rejection of mainstream patriotism.

The reaction to Ali joining the Nation of Islam was swift and harsh. Roy Wilkins, chairman of the NAACP, remarked, "Cassius may not know it, but he is now an honorary member of the White Citizens' Councils." Although he would later support Ali for his principled refusal to serve in the military in the Vietnam War, Martin Luther King Jr. publicly criticized Ali after his conversion to Islam: "When Cassius Clay joined the Black Muslims and started calling himself Cassius X he became a champion of racial segregation and that is what we are fighting against." Tapping into a long-standing just-shut-up-and-play trope reserved for athletes who make political statements, King continued, "I think perhaps Cassius should spend more time proving his boxing skill and do less talking." Others criticized Ali—and the Nation of Islam more generally—for not embracing the political struggle for civil rights.

On September 4, 1964, however, Federal Bureau of Investigation (FBI) wiretaps on King captured a conversation between the boxer and the civil rights leader in which they appeared to be on friendlier terms. The FBI log summed up the conversation between "C" and "MLK" this way: "MLK wished him well on his recent marriage, C invited MLK to be his guest at his next championship fight, MLK said he would like to attend. C said that he is keeping up with MLK that MLK is his brother, and with him 100% but can't take any chances, and that MLK should take care of himself, that MLK is known world wide and should watch out for them whities."

Being an athlete activist means catching flak. Journalists who once adored Ali turned against him, maligning the quirkiness they previously championed. They drew a sharp contrast between the Cassius Clay they liked—"The delightful Clay, the iambic poet, smiling broadly, jubilantly discussing himself"—and the Muhammad Ali they found troublesome—"a disciple of Malcolm X and Elijah Muhammad, leaders of the Black Muslims, a Negro racist movement." *Sports Illustrated* dismissed his religious conversion and all the hubbub surrounding it as "tragicomic nonsense." Columnist Jimmy Cannon claimed in *The New York Post* that Ali had turned boxing "into an instrument of hate" and "a weapon of wickedness." Boxer Floyd Patterson wrote in *Sports Illustrated* that "I can't respect him as a champion or as a man . . . He might just as well have joined the Ku Klux Klan."

Within a month of Ali's title-winning bout with Liston in 1964, the World Boxing Association (WBA) threatened to snatch away his title for post-fight actions that were "detrimental to boxing." Later, appearing at a Senate hearing, WBA president Ed Lassman contended Clay should be suspended "because he brags 'I am the greatest.'" But beyond the predominantly white boxing establishment, Ali was enormously popular as a symbol of independence that resonated with global freedom fighters like Nelson Mandela of South Africa. Ali also jumpstarted a boxing promotional company—Main Bout Inc.—designed to channel money toward Black athletes and promoters instead of the sport's white powerbrokers who were exploiting Black boxers.

Pressure on Ali only intensified with his refusal to participate in the Vietnam War. "I ain't got no quarrel with them Vietcong," he famously quipped. While his stance as a conscientious objector endeared Ali to the growing anti-war movement, the press was incredulous. *Time* magazine reported sarcastically, "it occurred to the champ after all these years that he 'might be a conscientious objector.'"

In 1967, after King had radicalized politically, Ali and the civil rights leader shared a private meeting in Louisville six days before King delivered his famous speech at Riverside Church in New York where he spoke out against "the giant triplets of racism, extreme materialism, and militarism" and called the US government "the greatest purveyor of violence in the world today." Weeks later in Atlanta, while speaking in front of his Ebenezer Baptist Church parish, he championed Ali's principled resistance to the war and received a standing ovation.

Meanwhile, after he failed two standardized intelligence tests, the Army lowered its passing scores and reclassified Ali as 1-A: eligible for duty. When Ali refused to report, the US Department of Justice prosecuted him for his declared conscientious-objector status. He was found guilty of violating Selective Service laws, and in June 1967, he was sentenced to five years in prison. In short, Ali paid a price for his political principles. His refusal to be drafted into the Vietnam War meant a ban from boxing. Although the US Supreme Court overturned Ali's conviction in June 1971, he missed more than three years in the prime of his boxing career. This decimated his income, forcing him to extend his boxing career to make up for lost earnings.

But, as Howard Bryant notes, "Ali was indomitable." He "had a second act after they tried to destroy him." Upon his return to the ring, he won, against all odds, that aforementioned fight versus George Foreman. He also fought three epic bouts against Joe Frazier, including the brutal "Thrilla in Manila" in 1975, where Ali somehow won back the heavyweight title. This, in turn, meant taking more blows in the ring—200,000 punches in all, according to one estimate—marking steps on the road to his eventual Parkinson's disease.

Fast-forward to 1996. Atlanta was hosting the Summer Olympics. At the opening ceremonies, as Beethoven's "Ode to Joy" boomed in the background, Muhammad Ali raised the Olympic torch with his right arm while his left hand quivered at his side, the Parkinson's disease he had long suffered writhing its way through his body. As Ali lit the wick that would zip diagonally up the guideline to the cauldron, Bob Costas remarked, "Once the most dynamic figure in sports, a gregarious man, now trapped inside that mask created by Parkinson's Syndrome." Co-host Dick Enberg said Ali was "arguably the most famous person on this earth." While all this was true, it was also an apolitical portrayal that subtly smothered Ali's complexity. Ali "had his political teeth extracted" that day, wrote his biographer Mike Marqusee.

Although the Atlanta Olympics cemented Ali's status as a world celebrity, sportswriter Dave Zirin points out that much more was in play: "Ali has been absorbed by the establishment as a legend—a harmless, helpful icon. There is barely a trace left of the ragged truth: Never has an athlete been more reviled by the mainstream press, more persecuted by the US government, or more defiantly beloved throughout the world than Muhammad Ali." Ali's narrow portrayal at the Atlanta Olympics made him legible to the barons of capital, and he took on sponsorship deals with the likes of Wheaties, Pizza Hut, Apple, Under Armour, and Toyota. This points to one of the perils of political activism: appropriation—or cooptation—whereby one's principles and history are watered down to meet the needs of others. For instance, in 2004, Adidas launched a $50-million ad campaign featuring the voice-over of Ali's daughter Laila saying, "Impossible is not a fact. It's an opinion. Impossible is not a declaration. It's a dare. Impossible is potential. Impossible is temporary. Impossible is nothing." As moving as the commercial may be, Ali's sharp political edges were sandpapered away.

But not everyone is keen to erase Muhammad Ali's principled politics. At Ali's funeral service in 2016, the Onondaga Nation Faithkeeper Oren Lyons recalled how Ali stood in solidarity with Native peoples when Congress wanted to terminate tribes in the 1970s. "Ali marched into Washington with us," he said. "He was a free, independent spirit, who stood his ground with great courage and conviction." Lyons concluded, "On his journey in life he lived and learned the hard way. He brought a light into this world . . . and that light will shine a long, long time."

BILLIEJEAN
KinG
FRENCH

BILLIE JEAN KING

"Even if you're not a born activist, life can damn sure make you one."

Billie Jean King (née Moffitt) wrote those words roughly eighty years after she came into the world, but something about her trailblazing life makes it seem they could have been on her mind from the start. Born during wartime on November 22, 1943, in Long Beach, California, Billie Jean quickly discovered there was an unavoidable conflict between her sense of drive and the buttoned-up sexism of American sports culture.

Long Beach, at the time, was a stronghold of fundamentalist churches, anticommunist vim, and staunch conservative vigor. Bill Moffitt, Billie Jean's father and namesake, could have represented the Long Beach hegemony on a poster. He was an ex-athlete, a sports lover, a veteran, a patriot, a professional firefighter, and the leader of a traditional patriarchal marriage. He took pride in being "boss, breadwinner, and the one who made all the final decisions." And even though he taught Billie Jean and her younger brother, Randy, to respect every individual no matter their background, he still indulged in flashes of racism, homophobia, and religious intolerance. He was, as Billie Jean's future husband would put it, "straight out of Archie Bunker." Bill was also a natural coach. On one hand, he could be "an unbelievable stickler on fundamentals and discipline." On the other, he would routinely lavish time and attention on his kids' pursuit of an athletic skill.

King's mother, Betty, embodied the classic mid-century stay-at-home mom. She enjoyed the arts, shopping, and discussing hairstyles. She tried unsuccessfully to share those interests with Billie Jean, who always "felt it was too bad she didn't have another girl around" who might have matched her enthusiasm. Still, Betty generously supported her children's pursuits. She was a tireless chauffeur and a faithful chaperone for constant practices and events. Despite King's many differences with her parents, she was proud of them. Their quirks, contradictions, and unflagging support helped shape the champion she would become, both on and off the tennis court.

One aspect of King's life that contained zero contradictions was her passion for athletics. From the start, she thrived on them. When Billie Jean finally got her hand on a tennis racket around age eleven, she almost never set it down. After her first lesson, she got into the family's 1947 Chevrolet convertible and told her mother, "I want to play tennis forever. I'm going to be the Number One tennis player in the whole world." Betty Moffitt's understated reply—"That's fine, dear"—was one thing. Billie Jean's precocious commitment to the idea was another. The family's backyard fence, for example, became her backstop for practicing strokes—until it disintegrated. Then, to take its place, Bill Moffitt wisely installed a cement wall, something that just might stand up to the constant pounding. He also presciently added a floodlight to allow for practicing in the dark.

While King had a deep love for the sport, her feelings about its prevailing culture were much different. A bastion of starched-collar, country-club classism, the tennis establishment existed as a web of rules and routines that enforced the status quo to the detriment of advancing the game. If you came from money and were a white man, excellent. If you came from money and knew your place as a lady, fine. But if you were someone with singular devotion to tennis and no tolerance for gender stereotyping and other arbitrary social gamesmanship, watch out. Naturally, King found herself repeatedly excluded and rebuffed by the tennis world, even as she climbed the rankings in her age groups. Wear shorts instead of a dress? You're out. Can't afford the ticket to Europe? You're out. Brimming with confident ambition? You're out. Again and again, the tennis world told Billie Jean King that she was unwelcome and did not belong.

At age thirteen, however, Billie Jean experienced an epiphany of perseverance—and it came in the tall, powerful form of tennis great Althea Gibson. While watching the Pacific Southwest Championships at the Los Angeles Tennis Club, King had the chance to see Gibson play. She sat enraptured by the tall, magisterial woman, who had recently swept the singles, doubles, and mixed doubles titles at Wimbledon. Gibson had already done for tennis what Jackie Robinson had done for baseball. But that day she also helped a thirteen-year-old dreamer imagine the kind of courage and tenacity a woman could muster to play tennis—maybe even changing the world in the process.

By the time King set off for college in 1961, she had already become an accomplished player, boasting a Wimbledon doubles title and a rank of third in the nation. Yet no schools offered her a scholarship, because at the time there were none for women. As a result, King became a commuter student at Los Angeles State College. She worked odd jobs to get by and relegated her competitive tennis schedule to summers. King's lack of a scholarship illustrates a central grievance that would later animate her activism around Title IX. Signed into law in 1972, Title IX mandated gender equity in any educational program receiving federal aid, including athletics. King became one of the law's most visible defenders, testifying before Congress, backing litigation to enforce compliance, and speaking out against institutional loopholes that threatened its reach. She once even called it the third most consequential piece of legislation in the 20th century, behind women receiving the vote and the Civil Rights Act. By lending her fame and unflinching voice, King ensured that Title IX had not just legal standing but cultural force enough to multiply women's participation in sports tenfold. But in order to lend fame to the cause, King first had to achieve it and to do so without the kind of financial support enjoyed by her male counterparts.

Even though she repeated as Wimbledon doubles champion in 1962 and made the Wimbledon singles final in 1963, losing to perennial champion Margaret Smith Court, King began to doubt whether she could continue as a self-supporting, part-time pro. And that's when she got The Call—that is, a telephone call from Australian businessman and famous tennis patron, Bob Mitchell. He was the main supporter of major players like Margaret Smith Court and Roy Emerson, the world's top male amateur. Mitchell offered to fly King to Melbourne and give her access to more world-class tennis training than she could handle. For someone who had always dreamed of becoming number one in the world, it was the offer of a lifetime. After being encouraged by her boyfriend and future husband, Larry, that he would wait for her and that she had to seize the chance to realize her full potential, King headed to Australia.

If life in the United States had been slowly molding King into an activist waiting for her moment, Australia rapidly forged her into a player who could become the world's number one. Finally, tennis became King's undivided focus. Pitted against the best competition, male and female, often two versus one, she gained new levels of skill and stamina. Although she had occasionally practiced together with men in college, King recalled that "for the most part, our American men—especially our best players—never thought to include us [female players] when they hit together. I thought it was wild that I had to travel to the other side of the world to find top-level men who were open-minded about female accomplishment and didn't mind training with me."

King's experience of an open-minded tennis community confirmed firsthand what she had always felt: there was a far better way to live and play and practice and compete than the sexist, segregated, hardscrabble system that American tennis players were forced to endure. She took that knowledge back to the United States, married Larry King in 1965, and went on a historic tear.

In 1966 she realized her childhood dream and earned the number one ranking in world tennis. That year, she also won her first Wimbledon singles title. Now that she was recognized as the top player, King felt a call to action. Her experiences in Australia and the political change and turmoil in the air during the early 1960s all told her it was time. The conviction and ambition King had felt at age thirteen while watching Althea Gibson was ready to bloom. Maybe she could translate her passion for tennis into change for the world.

And did she ever. With confidence and skill, she won Wimbledon again in 1967 and 1968. In 1970 she joined eight other female players in leaving the tennis establishment to start their own tour. Signing symbolic one-dollar contracts, the group—later dubbed the "Original 9"—launched the Virginia Slims Circuit with backing from tennis promoter Gladys Heldman and sponsorship from a cigarette brand that, while controversial, offered crucial financial independence. It was a revolutionary stand against the vast disparity in prize money and opportunity between men and women. As King later recalled, "We all felt like we were carrying the future of women's tennis onto the court each night." The tour's success forced the tennis world to reckon with women as both athletes and professionals.

In 1971 she again captured the singles title at Wimbledon, and 1972 proved even better. King took the singles titles at the US Open, the French Open, and Wimbledon and was both the first woman and the first tennis player to be named *Sports Illustrated*'s Sportsperson of the Year. She also called out the inequity in prize money for men and women, refusing to play at tournaments that did not put things right. In 1973 she helped women's tennis unionize, founding the Women's Tennis Association and serving as its first president. On the side, she found time to spearhead (and win) the "Battle of the Sexes," a singles match that pitted her against chauvinistic former champion Bobby Riggs. Seen by 90 million people around the world, the match became one of the few events in modern sports history with an impact far larger than its over-the-top spectacle. Not one to rest on her laurels, in 1974 King co-founded a co-ed professional tennis league and a magazine "dedicated to creating leaders by providing girls access to sports and to defending Title IX in lawsuits."

By her retirement from competitive play in 1983, King had amassed thirty-nine Grand Slam titles, third most in women's tennis history. She had also established herself as a cultural force. Her philanthropy, activism, and business endeavors continued to grow, and her significant endorsement portfolio supported those efforts. In 1981, however, King faced the type of scandal she had long feared. A former female lover filed a palimony suit against her. Rather than deny the affair, King publicly took responsibility for her infidelity. It was one of the first admissions to homosexuality by an American public figure. Companies immediately pulled her endorsements.

King lost millions. Hate mail poured in. Her husband, family, and businesses suffered. On top of everything, King faced the inner turmoil of worrying how to protect those she loved, along with all the good work she had started in the world. The turmoil, however, brought growth. It led King to "finally deal with lifelong struggles with eating disorders and internalized homophobia, and it also seems to have clarified for her the need to battle the sport's elitism in a more tactical and intentional way." Through the process, King became stronger and clearer than ever in her advocacy of the issues she had always championed. She also became one of the first and only public figures, let alone superstar athletes, to defend and represent LGBTQ rights.

"Sometimes I ask people to imagine themselves at the end of their life," King writes in her book, *All In*. "I say, *When you look at yourself in the mirror, when you're older and wrinkled like I am, how will you want to remember yourself? How will you want others to remember you? What will you want to say that you stood for, and did with your life?*"

King hasn't always had those answers ready-made. And that's the point. Her life shows that through a tenacious focus on doing right by oneself and others, a person can uncover powerful, personal ways of winning, giving, and being.

TOMMIE
FRENCH

TOMMIE SMITH

When Tommie Smith speared his gloved fist into the Mexico City sky at the 1968 Summer Olympics, he knew his political activism was putting his life at risk. In the months leading into the Games, the harassment rolled in thick and furious, including, he noted, "the threats on my life, the letters in the mail, the mock tickets back to Africa, all the different names they were calling us." Smith had a whirlwind of thoughts flitting through his mind as the 200-meter final began, including a leg injury he had sustained in the semifinal heat. Yet he conjured laser-like concentration and blazed his way to a gold medal in world-record time, despite throwing his hands in the air for the final ten meters.

But Smith would be forever etched into historical memory for the way he marked winning gold, with an unmistakable act of political dissent. He was joined by bronze medal winner John Carlos (see next chapter), who also thrust his clenched fist into the air during the playing of the national anthem. Together, they did not merely create an iconic snapshot from Olympic history—this was an indelible moment of world history.

And yet, Smith has insisted, the coordinated political act has often been misinterpreted. "This was not the Black Power movement. To this very day, the gesture made on the victory stand is described as a Black Power salute; it was not," he said. "Nor was it about black athletes talking about boycotting because they don't like what's going on. It was the Olympic Project for *Human Rights*." He added, "That gold medal had to be won by someone who really believed in the Olympic Project for Human Rights and the contention that it helped everybody, not just the black athletes."

Smith knew how to work hard to achieve a goal. When he was a child, Smith moved from Texas to Lemoore, California, where after a full day of school, followed by football practice, he would head to the fields to put in a shift picking crops like cotton, corn, and grapes. A PE teacher at Central Union school in Lemoore recognized Smith's talents and secured his father a job as head custodian so that young Tommie could continue to develop his running skills. Smith's father agreed to the proposition, but challenged his son to be the very best he could be: "If I ever find out you finished in second place—it's over," he told him. "You'll be back here working with us [in the fields]." Smith recounted, "What he told me lingered in my soul as a source of motivation for the rest of my life as an athlete, as a man." He added, "From that point forward, every time I lined up to race anyone, my goal would be to annihilate them."

Having seen what happened to outspoken Black leaders like Malcolm X and Martin Luther King Jr., he knew that there were real risks in making a firm political stand in public. As a student at San Jose State University, he participated in a march from San Jose to San Francisco for racial justice, so his actions in Mexico City were rooted in experience.

To be sure, Smith paid a high price for his protest in Mexico City. Olympic officials ejected him and Carlos from the Olympic Village. Once he returned to the United States, jobs were hard to come by. He lost his marriage to the pressure and stress. His relationship with Carlos strained. The Australian sprinter Peter Norman, who had won silver and who wore an Olympic Project for Human Rights button in solidarity on the medal stand, was also treated like a pariah in his home country. At the Sydney Olympics in 2000, Norman was willfully ignored by Games organizers even though he was the country's most successful sprinter.

The athlete activists were pilloried in the press as well. Arthur Daley slammed them in *The New York Times*: "Smith and Carlos brought their world smack into the Olympic Games, where it did not belong, and created a shattering situation that shook this international sports carnival to its very core." Brent Musburger, writing for the *Chicago American*, raged against the "black-skinned storm troopers" he viewed as "unimaginative blokes." He fulminated, "One gets a little tired of having the United States run down by athletes who are enjoying themselves at the expense of their country. Protesting and working constructively against racism in the United States is one thing, but airing one's dirty clothing before the entire world during a fun-and-games tournament was no more than a juvenile gesture by a couple of athletes who should have known better."

But Smith and Carlos had ardent supporters who viewed their act not as a "juvenile gesture" but rather as courageous, principled dissent. Jesse Jackson, who at the time was working with the Southern Christian Leadership Conference, wrote a telegram directly to Tommie Smith congratulating him for his bravery, stating, "You may have been on the wrong side of the Olympic Committee, but on the right side of history." He then issued Smith an open invitation to come speak at the group's community meetings, expenses paid. One person from Los Angeles wrote a letter to IOC President Avery Brundage to condemn "the senseless, idiotic, racist reaction of our Olympic Committee." He concluded that the athletes "will be greeted as black power heroes by an incensed black America, more convinced than ever that white America has nothing but hatred for the black man." He ended his letter vowing to donate to the Urban League "in the hopes that they can achieve brotherhood in the world, since you have so badly failed."

In the rearview mirror of history, the courage that Smith and Carlos demonstrated on the medal stand and beyond tends to be celebrated. When President Barack Obama welcomed Olympic and Paralympic athletes to the White House after the 2016 Summer Olympics in Rio, he included Smith and Carlos. Obama said that he wanted to "take a minute to thank some people who paved the way to create that sense that we're in this together. We're honored to have the legendary Tommie Smith and John Carlos here today." While those in attendance erupted in applause, he added, "Proud of them. Their powerful silent protest in the 1968 Games was controversial, but it woke folks up and created greater opportunity for those that followed."

In 2019, more than fifty years after the US Olympic Committee bent to the prejudiced whims of International Olympic Committee President Avery Brundage and dislodged Smith and Carlos from the Olympic Village, the US Olympic Committee inducted the athletes into its Hall of Fame. A black-and-white photograph of the men is also on display at the Smithsonian National Museum of African American History and Culture in Washington, DC. They have been vindicated by history.

Smith has forever stood by the politics that he espoused in 1968. "God had a plan for me," he wrote. "I hold no regrets." And he has voiced support for modern-day athlete activists who have taken political stands, people like Mahmoud Abdul-Rauf and LeBron James. Smith has also openly backed Colin Kaepernick, stating, "Don't hate the kid because he stood up for something to change. He stood up for the right to exercise Amendment 1." He has appeared in public donning an "I'M WITH KAP" T-shirt. Tommie Smith understands as well as anyone what solidarity means.

JOHN

JOHN CARLOS

John Carlos has long understood the power of collective action. At the 1968 Olympics, he and Tommie Smith stood on the medal stand after winning bronze and gold in the 200-meter dash and thrust their fists skyward as the national anthem played. They were protesting the poverty and racism that afflicted the United States and the wider world. Carlos did this, he later said, "To set a standard. To bring attention to the plight of people who were less fortunate. To wake up the consciousness of those who had let their conscience go dormant. And to encourage people to stand for what's right."

The action was deliberately symbolic. "We decided that we would wear black gloves to represent strength and unity," Carlos stated. "We would have beads hanging from our neck, which would represent the history of lynching. We wouldn't wear shoes to symbolize the poverty that still plagued so much of black America. On the medal stand, all we would wear on our feet would be black socks." Carlos also left his jacket open to represent his working-class roots. Silver medalist Peter Norman of Australia stood by in solidarity. All three men pinned human-rights buttons on their track jackets.

But Carlos and Smith's activist circle was wider than that human trifecta that is now engraved in Olympic history. They were part of a group called the Olympic Project for Human Rights. The OPHR emerged in 1967 as a space where athletes—and allies like sociology professor Harry Edwards—could discuss and reflect upon their experiences working in sporting spaces that were rippling with racialized oppression. In

December 1967, the OPHR issued six demands, including the "restoration of Muhammad Ali's title and right to box in this country," the dismissal of the International Olympic Committee President Avery Brundage, and the banning of all-white sports teams from apartheid-era South Africa and Southern Rhodesia (Zimbabwe). Ahead of the Olympics, numerous athletes, including Carlos, even threatened to boycott the 1968 Games if South Africa were allowed to participate. He was joined by fellow track-star Olympian Lee Evans and supported by prominent sports figures like Arthur Ashe, Jim Bouton, Wilt Chamberlain, and Jackie Robinson. Months of activist campaigning—often led by athletes themselves—built up to Smith and Carlos's act of defiance. Movements created space for the athletes' unforgettable act of dissent.

John Carlos was born and raised in New York City, where he witnessed the positive effects of the Harlem Renaissance firsthand. He grew up in a working-class household in Harlem: his father was a shoemaker while his mother was a nurse's aide at Bellevue Hospital. At a young age, Carlos became accustomed to the money hustle, engaging in an array of activities, from busking with friends outside the Savoy Ballroom to breaking into freight trains and making off with boxes of food that he would share with the community. When not Robin-Hooding, he was active with sports. His first love was swimming. Carlos even won the New York City 200-meter freestyle championship and aspired to swim at the Olympics until his father gave him a "'come to Jesus' talk," explaining that African Americans did not have access to the swimming pools that could take him to the next level. Racism dashed his dreams of swimming, but it didn't stop him from pursuing track, in which he excelled and quickly gained the attention of college coaches.

All the while, Carlos was political. As a teenager, he trailed Malcolm X through Harlem, watching him speak whenever he could. "It was like he was blowing out my eardrums without raising his voice," Carlos wrote in his autobiography. "His power, and the response of the audience, grew out of the fact that he was articulating ideas we were thinking about all the time but didn't really have a language or vocabulary to express. For me, it was like he grabbed onto my frustrations and turned them into logic." From Malcolm X he also learned to attack injustice head-on. Carlos organized a boycott of the school cafeteria to gain improvements in the quality of the food. When his landlord was pocketing government funds that he was supposed to use to eradicate insects, Carlos torched the trees, setting them ablaze so his mother could sit outside without being harassed by caterpillars. The experiences taught him that "You don't just get in trouble for doing something bad or wrong. You can also get in trouble because you stand up for ideas and principles that challenge people in power."

That is precisely what happened at the 1968 Mexico City Olympics: Carlos stood up to the powerful even if that meant receiving punishment and scorn. Carlos and Smith's glove-clad hands quickly became lightning rods for media heat. One *New York Times* columnist railed against the athletes as "divisive" and characterized their dissent as "disgraceful, insulting, and embarrassing." IOC President Brundage was livid. He pressured the US Olympic Committee to suspend the athletes from the team and dismiss them from the Olympic Village. The USOC complied, releasing a statement that read in part, "The United States Olympic Committee expresses its profound regrets to the International Olympic Committee, to the Mexican Organizing Committee and to the people of Mexico for the discourtesy displayed by two members of its team in departing from tradition during a victory ceremony at the Olympic Stadium." The response underlines what sociologist Ben Carrington calls "the fear of the black athlete" as rooted in "the projection of white masculinist fantasies of domination [and] control."

The backlash against Carlos and Smith was ferocious. As scholar Douglas Hartmann points out, they were portrayed in the press as "villains or traitors, and described in emotionally charged language usually reserved for the most violent and threatening figures Americans could possibly imagine: terrorists, communists, even Nazi storm troopers." Money was scarce. Carlos describes chopping up his furniture to use as firewood. Both he and his wife Kim suffered from depression. She eventually took her own life.

Carlos never backtracked from his iconic medal-stand activism. And, as we noted in the previous chapter, history has been kind to Carlos and his comrades. Even President Barack Obama publicly praised Carlos and Smith: "I think to signify in that Olympics that there was more work to do, to acknowledge the injustices that were still taking place, I think that was a breakthrough moment in an overall push to move this country towards a more equal and more just society." Obama added, "I think that what they did was in the best tradition of American protest."

WYOMIA
TYUS
FRENCH

WYOMIA TYUS

In 2020, multiple generations of Black women athletes gathered online to speak about the past, present, and future of Black women's athlete activism. The women represented a variety of sports at all different levels. While most of the athletes were actively playing or had competed in the last decade, Wyomia Tyus stood alone as the titan and torchbearer of the field. The 1964 and 1968 Olympian was showered with respect by athlete activists who walked in her footsteps. One panelist and future Olympian, Anna Cockrell, had written her MA thesis on Tyus's career and activism. Gwen Berry, who at the time was garnering headlines for her protests, saw a straight line between her activism and what Tyus had done years before. "I feel there is a direct connection between us," Berry said. "It's unfortunate we don't hear these stories. So often, women are overlooked. We bear the biggest burdens."

Tyus was born on August 29, 1945, in the Jim Crow South. She was raised with three older brothers in Griffin, Georgia, where her father worked as a dairy farmer and her mother labored as a laundress. Tyus grew up chasing after her brothers, playing sports in the neighborhood, and showing early signs of the track star she would eventually become. While life in a town where the Ku Klux Klan held regular rallies was not perfect, for Tyus it still offered possibility and promise. Yet when she was a teenager, her family's house burned down. This life-altering event exacted a particularly heavy toll on her father, and he passed away shortly after.

Tyus was devastated. Withdrawing into herself, she turned to sports as a release. She would run faster and faster but talk less and less. Track was an escape for Tyus, but it would soon become a vehicle to a new life. Recruited by legendary coach Ed Temple to run with the storied Tennessee State University track team, the Tigerbelles, Tyus soon found herself in Nashville. At a time when most colleges were not investing in competitive athletic programs for women, Black schools in the South stood out for the opportunities they provided for women athletes. Tennessee State offered summer training camps, scholarships, and travel opportunities.

In many ways, Tennessee State and the Tigerbelles became Tyus's portal to the world. Through track competitions, she began to travel. Sport took Tyus around the world and introduced her to new ideas and possibilities. In the 1960s, the spirit of protest and upheaval was palpable, and not just in the United States. As global decolonization efforts produced newly independent nation-states and the United States and the Soviet Union faced off in the Cold War, every trip provided a window to an ever-changing world and a chance for Tyus to find her place in it.

Before she even began college, Tyus was invited to join a team competing in a track meet in the Soviet Union. These dual meets were Cold War concoctions in which track athletes from the United States and Russia would compete directly. Not surprisingly, each country attached political importance to these meets, hoping to earn bragging rights that would validate the political and economic philosophies of each respective country. Athletes like Tyus were caught in the web of these global tensions.

Tyus recalls how eye-opening it was to travel on these trips. From people trying to rub her skin off because they were curious about Black people to seeing the ruins and remnants of war in Poland, new opportunities abounded. "I think my eyes must have stayed open the entire time," Tyus wrote in her memoir. While she was there to race, the geopolitics that brought her there were never far away. Journalists reported the results of the dual meets as matters of national interest. The stakes were high. One third-place finish resulted in headlines and articles decrying how the American women could not compete with the Russians. For a teenaged Tyus, these travels were educational in more than one way.

In 1964 Tyus went to Tokyo to compete in her first Olympic Games. These travels only expanded her fascination with the world. The chance to mix and mingle with athletes who ate different food, spoke different languages, and experienced the world differently was profoundly impactful. One thing that deeply resonated was how different Japan felt from Georgia. During some downtime at the Olympics, Tyus went shopping with teammates. At the department store, the Japanese salespeople helped them try on shoes. In the segregated South, Black people were not allowed to sample shoes in department stores. These experiences shaped Tyus's view of what was possible in the world.

After winning gold in the 100-meter dash at the 1964 Olympics, Tyus returned to Georgia. She simultaneously found herself feeling visible and invisible. A parade was thrown in her honor in her hometown of Atlanta but only went through the Black part of town. The White House hosted a visit to celebrate Olympians, but subsequent reporting only mentioned the male athletes by name. Back at Tennessee State, it was "college as usual" for Tyus and the other Tigerbelles. Tyus was reaching places she never thought she would go and experiencing things she could have hardly dreamed of, and yet there was a lingering feeling that, for all the ways she was growing and things she was accomplishing, she still wasn't being fully *seen*.

As part of the US Department of State's Cold War propaganda efforts, Black jazz musicians, artists, and athletes were sought after to perform globally as "goodwill ambassadors." These sponsored trips sought to counter critiques of American race relations and develop relationships with newly independent nation-states, particularly in Africa. Tyus was selected for a trip to East Africa that would take her through Tanzania, Mozambique, Kenya, and Ethiopia. While the State Department had its own agenda, Tyus used this opportunity to continue to travel and learn. "It gave me a big appreciation for people, for my people, for people who look like me," Tyus wrote. "Being able to be there and understand . . . and through that understanding, improve on who I was as a person." Back in the United States, Tyus's understanding of the African diaspora and Black liberation politics continued to develop. In 1967, she was impacted by a speech that movement leader Stokely Carmichael delivered in Nashville. "[He] reminded us that we were human beings, that we were no longer slaves and that we had to be more active." And that is exactly what Tyus did.

By the time the 1968 Mexico City Summer Olympics rolled around, some Black athletes had become increasingly vocal about Black liberation globally. Out in San Jose, California, Dr. Harry Edwards and a handful of athletes, including Tommie Smith and John Carlos, had started the Olympic Project for Human Rights (OPHR). Members of the OPHR raised the possibility of a Black American Olympic boycott and were vocally opposed to the International Olympic Committee's inclusion of South Africa and Rhodesia at the upcoming Olympics. In the lead-up to the Games, the OPHR debated the best approach to take, holding meetings to unify concerned athletes. Yet they never reached out or included Black women athletes in these conversations.

As the sporting world gathered in Mexico for the 1968 Games, the undercurrent of protest was palpable. Tyus and her teammates had enough of being sidelined and made sure to include themselves in all meetings about possible demonstrations. Ultimately it was decided, however, that athletes would express their political concerns individually rather than participate in a coordinated group effort.

At her first event, the 100-meter competition, Tyus approached the blocks and performed the "Tighten Up" dance from Archie Bell & the Drells' popular R&B song at the time. Wearing black shorts as her protest, rather than the Team USA-issued white shorts, Tyus flew out of the blocks, and as she crossed the finish line, she raised one fist. "This is how I decided I would protest," Tyus explained. "The shorts were at the forefront of my whole being to bring attention to human rights, whether anybody picked that up or not." In winning the gold medal in the 100-meter event, she became the first athlete ever—male or female, Black or white—to be a repeat winner in that event.

While other athletes engaged in their own protest, the medal-stand pose by sprinters Tommie Smith and John Carlos quickly overshadowed the actions and accolades of their teammates, including Tyus. Yet Tyus was undeterred and determined to continue to raise her voice—and now to also amplify her support of Smith and Carlos. As the swift and severe fallout from Smith and Carlos's protest commenced, the media and the US Olympic Committee attempted to paint a picture of Smith and Carlos as rogue athletes. One newspaper stated that "not even the black women on their team supported them." Following the women's gold in the 4×100-meter relay, Tyus immediately corrected the record, dedicating their medals to Smith and Carlos in an act of solidarity. Her actions sent a clear message of support and solidarity, thereby quashing the narrative of a divided Black track team.

Tyus was not the only one dedicating medals. In the same room, a representative of the Cuban women's relay team also declared they were dedicating their medals to "Stokely Carmichael" and the larger Black Power movement. All the women on the relay team were Afro-Cuban. Both medal dedications, as well as Tyus's earlier protest, have been often overlooked in the accounts of the 1968 Games and in histories of athletic activism. This has obscured both the achievements and direct protests of Tyus and other Black women athletes and left them virtually silenced as political participants at the 1968 Games and beyond.

Following the 1968 Olympics, Tyus found herself frustrated with the lack of opportunities as a woman athlete. There were no professional pathways, few coaching jobs, and little pay. "She had thought she had done everything right," wrote Jennifer Lansbury. "Yet despite her gold medals, world records, *and* college degree, Wyomia Tyus could not find a job that paid her a respectable salary." Tyus became an outspoken advocate for women's sports. Joining Billie Jean King and other notable women athletes, she helped to start the Women's Sports Foundation. She worked as a coach in Los Angeles and participated in panels, events, and organizations that were working to support women's equality in sport. Tyus has remained committed to that work for decades. It's what brought her into conversation with the next generation of Black women athlete activists.

"My dad used to say, 'You always have to stay in the fight,'" Tyus told a reporter in 2021. "I have tried to maintain that. And I think that all the women, from Gwen Berry on—they are standing for things that will make this a better world in which to live for everybody, not just for one group of people."

In recent years, Tyus has finally begun to be recognized as a trailblazer and activist. While she has appreciated the renewed attention, she also wanted to make sure she was the author of her own history. By publishing her memoir, *Tigerbelle*, Tyus found the words she was searching for decades earlier. Her story is not only a remarkable account of an early athlete activist but also a bridge that connects generations and offers a roadmap to a much longer and expansive history of athletic activism. As she reminds us at the end of her memoir, "Even if it feels sometimes like things are moving backward, you can't give up . . . You have to start the fire again, gather up all the little sparks and hope that, this time, the sparks come together."

MAHMOUD
ABDUL
RAUF
FRENCH

MAHMOUD ABDUL-RAUF

Most American children with Tourette syndrome are diagnosed around age seven. For Mahmoud Abdul-Rauf, who was then named Chris Jackson, the diagnosis didn't come until he was seventeen. This delayed recognition meant that, for much of his early life, Jackson was left managing his condition without insight, support, medical resources, or the simple reassurance he was not alone. His uncontrollable tics—blinking, twitching, and jerking movements—were accompanied by compulsive thoughts, lapses in consciousness, and even the occasional full-body collapse. His peers mocked him. His teachers, at one point, placed him in special education. But their treatments were gentle next to what he later called his "torturous self-deprecation and drive to perfectionism."

Raised by a single mother in an impoverished, crime-stricken area of Gulfport, Mississippi, Jackson seemed to have almost everything stacked against him. He would later realize, however, that his greatest apparent challenge, Tourette's, was also a secret superpower. His compulsiveness, perfectionism, and sense of desperation made him relentless. He would spend hours repeating the same dribble move or jump shot. And if something felt off in the slightest, it could lead to starting the whole routine over.

Jackson often competed against an "invisible man," an opponent who demanded more precision and speed with every possession. He drilled in the dark of dawn, sometimes in torrential downpours and lightning storms, oblivious to the toll on his body. Sometimes, in order to end a session, he would throw the basketball as far as he could toward home. Nothing less drastic would let him escape the commanding urge to do a drill again, even more perfectly.

Despite the intense demands of his work ethic on the court, basketball gave Jackson what Tourette's had denied him everywhere else: a sense of control. On the court, the jerks and tics could fade into the rhythm of the game. The ball was an anchor and the hoop a fixed point in a world that otherwise seemed uncertain. "As early as fourth grade, I decided it was basketball or death," he would later write. By the time Jackson reached high school, even though he was maybe 6'1" and 155 pounds, his countless hours of solitary practice had transformed him into a phenom. He became known as "The Mississippi Son" and won the state's Player of the Year twice over.

During his senior year at Gulfport High, Jackson was one of the most sought-after recruits in the nation. Almost every big-name program courted him, but he chose Louisiana State University because of the down-to-earth honesty and fairness he sensed in coach Dale Brown. At LSU he would quickly gain the nickname "Action Jackson," a nod to his breakneck pace, supersonic shot release, and uncanny ability to put a game into overdrive at will.

As a freshman in 1988–89, he rewrote the record books, setting NCAA freshman marks for points in a season (965), scoring average (30.2), and consecutive free throws (28). He made nearly every postseason All-America first team and appeared on the cover of *Sports Illustrated*. The next year, even alongside future NBA star Shaquille O'Neal, he again led the Southeastern Conference (SEC) in scoring average (27.8) and repeated as Player of the Year. By the 1990 NBA draft, "Action Jackson" was a household name, celebrated for pairing electrifying showmanship with clinical efficiency.

The Denver Nuggets made Jackson the third overall pick in the 1990 NBA Draft, drawn to his relentless offensive mindset, his unique potential on the court, and his inspiring backstory. In Jackson's first two years, he played off the bench, averaging 14 and then 10 points per game while adjusting to the speed and physicality of the NBA. During those years, he also continued a reading habit sparked by Dale Brown at LSU. Engrossed by *The Autobiography of Malcolm X* and then the Qur'an, Jackson began exploring deep themes of identity and morality. Those books, along with long hours of solitary reflection, drew him to Islam. In 1991, at 22 years old, he embraced the faith and quietly began incorporating its teachings into his daily life.

Two years later, Jackson made the change public by adopting the name Mahmoud Abdul-Rauf. While some in the basketball world warned that the Arabic name could hurt his marketability, Nuggets fans embraced it, chanting "Rauf, Rauf, Rauf is on fire!" during home games. For Abdul-Rauf, his new name was the declaration of a new identity, one grounded in spiritual conviction and a sense of accountability to something higher than his own immediate interests or that of the game to which he had dedicated most of his life. "God has given me, through His blessing, Tourette's," he said in 1994. "And He has given me basketball and Islam to cope with Tourette's. Through basketball, I get a little peace. And through Islam I get total peace."

This expanding intellectual and spiritual world paralleled the growth of his game. By the 1992–93 season, now firmly entrenched as the Nuggets' starting point guard, Abdul-Rauf was averaging 19.2 points per game—production that placed him among the league's most elite scorers at his position. He was becoming a fixture in nightly highlight reels, and Denver fans began to dream of glory under their new talisman. At the same time, Abdul-Rauf was reading more than ever before: works by Noam Chomsky, Howard Zinn, and Randall Robinson; accounts of slavery, colonialism, Jim Crow, and segregation; histories of America's foreign and domestic policies. The reading unsettled him and stirred a growing awareness of his complicated position as an American, a Black man, and a follower of Islam. These cross-currents—growing public expectation and deepening private conviction—were about to collide and form what would become a landmark in the history of American sports activism.

Early in the 1995–96 season, Abdul-Rauf adopted the practice of remaining in the locker room during the pregame national anthem. For months, neither the team nor the league objected. Then, in early March 1996, fans called a local sports radio show to complain. Within days, a *Denver Post* reporter asked why he would refuse to stand for a symbol of freedom and democracy. Mirroring the parallelism of the reporter's leading question, Abdul-Rauf replied that for many people in the world the flag was a symbol of tyranny and oppression.

That afternoon, the NBA suspended him indefinitely without pay for violating a league operations manual rule that players must "stand and line up in a dignified posture" for the anthem even though the Players Association noted the rule had never been collectively bargained. The *Denver Post* ran a poll showing 72 percent of local fans opposed his stance, many citing his $2.6 million salary as reason he should "be grateful." Abdul-Rauf, unfazed, told reporters, "My beliefs are more important than anything. If I have to give up basketball, I will."

The league and Abdul-Rauf soon reached a compromise. He would be present for the anthem, but it would be on his own terms. "I'll stand," Abdul-Rauf explained, "but I'll offer a prayer, my own prayer, for those who are suffering. Muslim. Caucasian. African-American. Asian. Whoever is in that position, whoever is experiencing difficulties." This agreement ended the suspension after one game, but the damage was done. In the court of public opinion, he had been branded as ungrateful, unpatriotic, and, of all things, foreign. Media coverage often collapsed his African American identity into a crude caricature of a Middle Eastern "outsider." Cartoonist Drew Litton's satirical sketches in the *Rocky Mountain News* "Arabized" his features, giving him a hooked nose, sunken eyes, and a longer beard. Hate mail poured in—two garbage bags' worth—much of it ordering him to "Go home!" or "Go back to Africa!"

Within months of his suspension, the Denver Nuggets traded Abdul-Rauf to the Sacramento Kings. Though just twenty-seven and still in his athletic prime, his minutes and visibility were slashed. After an injury-riddled 1997–98 season, the Kings left him unsigned. The Mississippi Son was essentially out of the league. He played in Turkey and then Italy before resurfacing for a single season with the Vancouver Grizzlies in the 2000–2001 season, but insiders widely reported the belief that his protest in Denver was the beginning of the end for his career. Sports sociologist Harry Edwards had long warned that outspoken Black athletes were tolerated only so long as they served the entertainment needs of the institution. Abdul-Rauf's NBA story is case in point.

What began as a private act of conscience had flared into a standoff between personal integrity and group conformity. Unfortunately for Abdul-Rauf, his protest unfolded during what Edwards has described as a long period of stagnation in Black athlete activism, stretching from the 1970s until the mid-2000s. This was an era without the mass mobilizations, coalition support, and movement infrastructure that had once shielded figures like Muhammad Ali or that would decades later aid Colin Kaepernick. At the time, there was no organized political or cultural force to amplify Abdul-Rauf's message, to contextualize his dissent, or to protect him from institutional reactions.

Abdul-Rauf tried to defend his position on constitutional grounds, emphasizing that his refusal to stand was protected under the First Amendment's guarantees of freedom of speech and religion. But that argument quickly ran aground against the NBA's contractual authority over player conduct. In the general press and public imagination, his legal reasoning was drowned out by the culture-war frame of loyalty versus ingratitude. As Zareena Grewal observes, it took only days for Abdul-Rauf's life story—once framed as the quintessential American dream, rising from poverty and disability to NBA stardom—to be recast as an "un-American" tale of angry entitlement. The same personal qualities once celebrated as grit and determination were reinterpreted as arrogance and militancy. Public backlash and the league's fear of alienating fans and sponsors combined to effectively undercut what promised to be a high-flying career.

In the years since, Abdul-Rauf has rebuilt his life, not around the prestige of the NBA but rather atop the principles that once cost him his place there. Besides playing in international leagues, and even starring in the Big3 into his late forties, he has traveled widely, speaking to audiences about discipline, faith, and the courage to act on conviction. He mentors young athletes, especially those working through how to live with integrity amidst the cultural and financial pressures of professional sports. To them and to many more, he is both a cautionary tale and a beacon, a living testament to the costs and rewards of staying true to one's convictions. As for those who still question his intentions, his commitments, or what he stands for: "Listen, I don't care what you or anybody else thinks," he once told a reporter. "I've made a decision that I'm going to live and die with a free conscience and a free soul, whether you or anybody likes it or not."

GWEN
BERRY
FRENCH

GWEN BERRY

When Gwen Berry stepped onto the podium at the 2019 Pan American Games in Lima, Peru, thoughts were swirling through her head. Her eyes closed, her gold medal from the hammer throw dangling from her neck, she swayed as the US national anthem played.

As the song neared its end, Berry had an epiphany. "At the last part—'land of the free and home of the brave'—something just came over me," she explained later. The anthem felt more like an unfulfilled promise, its lyrics ignoring the realities of America through Berry's eyes, through the eyes of a Black woman. Berry did not feel free, but she did feel brave. She bowed her head and raised her fist into the air. US fencer Race Imboden also protested at those same Games by taking a knee, a symbol of dissent popularized by NFL quarterback Colin Kaepernick three years earlier.

The image of Berry on the medal stand—raised fist, bright blue lipstick, defiant stance—quickly went viral. It harkened to the 1968 Olympic medal-stand protest by John Carlos and Tommie Smith. Her action became a fresh entry in the ongoing and increasingly vocal debate about sports and politics.

Berry's path to that podium had multiple origin points. Growing up, Berry played many sports, showing a knack for basketball. She started using track and field to improve her conditioning and agility for basketball. By the end of high school, however, Berry's success in track and field earned her a scholarship to Southern Illinois University Carbondale. With basketball in her rearview and track and field shaping her future, Berry headed off to college to develop as a thrower.

Berry's athletic growth was immediate and clear. From 2008 onward, she would break records and win medals, earning a place on the Olympic team en route to that top podium spot at the 2019 Pan American Games. Simultaneously, however, Berry was developing her social consciousness—a deeply personal journey that emerged publicly during her medal-stand protest, but that began five years earlier in 2014.

Prior to 2014 many Americans had never heard of Ferguson, Missouri. Yet by the end of that year, the suburb of St. Louis would be the epicenter of national news. On August 9, 2014, 18-year-old Michael Brown was shot and killed by police officer Darren Wilson. In the weeks that followed, Ferguson erupted in protests, reigniting a grassroots movement for Black lives and liberation that shifted discourse on police brutality and thrust the quiet suburb into the national spotlight. But for Gwen Berry, Ferguson was simply home.

Berry had grown up in a bustling household filled with a tight-knit multi-generational family. Berry's paternal family was very close and committed to collectively raising her while her dad was off playing college football and trying out for professional teams and later when he enlisted in the military and was deployed to Iraq. When Gwen had her own son at 15, her family was there to support her and baby Derrick, encouraging her to stay in school and pursue her educational and athletic dreams. She was shaped by her family and by Ferguson, and she carried both with her as her athletic career took off.

So in 2014, when Berry heard about Michael Brown's death and saw the news coming out of Ferguson, it broke her heart and sparked something inside of her. "Mike Brown, he was in my community," Berry explained, "he was probably friends with my cousins, you know? I'm from the area where he was slain. We walked the same streets, we went to the same parties."

Berry flew home from training to join her family and community in protest. She walked the streets while reflecting on her home and experiences and pondering what it meant to live as a Black American. "It definitely woke me up," Berry said. "I just had to look at myself and say, 'This could be my child. This could be my brother. This could be my uncle.'"

Steeled with a fresh sense of purpose, Berry headed to Oxford, Mississippi, to train at Ole Miss. While there, she took the opportunity to read about Black history, touring civil rights sites and nearby plantations, and attending Saturday morning Freedom Schools where she learned about community organizing. The original Freedom School model started in Mississippi in 1964 during Freedom Summer when civil rights organizers envisioned programs that would give Black youth a historically driven, politically engaged education geared toward helping them "articulate their own desires, demands, and questions" and "find alternative and ultimately new directions for action."

By the time Berry arrived at the 2019 Pan American Games, she had grown as an athlete as well as an activist. After winning gold in the hammer throw, she stepped onto the podium. The day before had been the five-year anniversary of Michael Brown's murder. She thought about Brown and other victims of police brutality. She thought about her son, who was now fifteen. She thought about her dad and his experiences as a Black veteran. She reflected on her Freedom School discussions, and she remembered the feeling of walking on plantations. The anthem's lyrics playing in her head felt hypocritical. With head bowed, she raised her fist. "I used that moment, my moment, to let my voice be heard without having to say anything at all."

As the clip of her protest went viral, many people supported Berry. But the backlash was also severe. Berry was placed on a 12-month probation by the US Olympic Committee for violating the IOC's Rule 50, which prohibits athletes from political demonstrations. She was subject to media-fueled hate campaigns and lost financial supporters and endorsement deals. Berry was at risk of leaving the sport until the racial justice organization Color of Change stepped in and sponsored her. Nine months into her probation, however, the world changed.

In May 2020, George Floyd's murder by police officer Derek Chauvin in Minneapolis ushered in a moment of collective reflection and action. It was not the first time a Black death went viral. Nor was it the first time that people took to the streets in protest. However, the way white America responded was noticeably different. Suddenly a national conversation on race and racism was taking shape. Brands and organizations, including the US Olympic and Paralympic Committee (USOPC), rushed to put out statements declaring "Black Lives Matter" and purporting to stand against racism.

Berry watched as US Olympic powerbrokers said the very things that led to her being placed on probation. She watched as the brands that had distanced themselves from her over the last year rushed to tweet #BlackLivesMatter. The USOPC acceded to Berry's demand and issued a public apology. It also rescinded her probation and announced it would no longer punish athletes or restrict their political protests. Puma even signed on to sponsor her, plugging her into an athlete-activist marketing campaign called "She Moves Us." The "great racial awakening" in 2020 was a moment in time, and a moment that was fleeting.

The 2020 Olympics were pushed to 2021 due to the COVID-19 pandemic. Berry headed into the US Olympic Trials determined to make the Olympic team again. After placing third and securing a spot on the squad, she walked to the medal stand to celebrate with her teammates. As she took the podium, however, a curious thing happened: the US anthem started to play. At US trials the anthem is customarily played only once at the beginning of competition. Yet, here in the middle of the day, at precisely the point Berry stepped onto the podium, it began to play. For Berry, it felt intentional that she was being targeted. It also felt like a test. Once again, she bowed her head. Reaching for her shirt that said "Activist Athlete," Berry held it up high as she turned away from the flag.

What followed was an organized hate campaign, fueled by right-wing journalists and politicians who called for Berry to be kicked off the team. Social media platforms allowed anonymous posters to proliferate hate. "As quickly as the world changed after George Floyd, it snapped back to normal," she lamented later.

Berry was clear: the world may have "changed the channel" on talking about racism, but she did not have that luxury. "Part of the reason I speak out is to make people uncomfortable," Berry explained, "I really want people to pay attention not just to me, but also to what I stand for. Being an Olympian, it's not just about *what* I represent, but *who* I'm representing. Who I'm speaking for. Who I'm a reflection of. When I stand on that podium, I am a reflection of teenage mothers. I am a reflection of Black women. I am a reflection of everyone who has had to overcome poverty."

Berry carried her message to the Olympic Games where she finished 11th in the hammer throw. She remains committed to using her podiums and platforms for raising awareness and advocating for social justice. "I am exhausted but exhilarated," Berry said. "I am happy that my message is getting out there. That's the point. If you see me, you have to see my people, and the issues I'm speaking to. You may not see them, but at the Olympics, you will see me . . . My protest isn't important, but my meaning is. That's my purpose. That's my peace. That's my joy."

ADVOCATES

REFRAME

Advocates challenged cultural and political status quos, trailblazing new paradigms of power and social engagement.

RUSSELL
BILL
BOSTON
6
FRENCH

BILL RUSSELL

The lines that define a sport cannot define an athlete. The starting line, the baseline, the goal line, the three-point line, even the monetary bottom line—these markers mean nothing when compared to the line of integrity that the greatest athletes draw within themselves and defend fiercely. It is this line, a standard of self-respect and moral clarity, that often guides society's and sport's most impactful heroes.

If the sentiment above seems right, if it rings true, that's doubtless in part because we live in a culture that has been shaped by the life and legacy of Boston Celtics legend Bill Russell. While other early athlete activists took stands and made arguments about social justice in terms of faith, or human rights, or fairness, Bill Russell rooted his powerful, personal activism in a conviction that social justice was well served when individuals courageously defended their own worth and dignity.

Russell learned this way of being from his family. As a "rural black guy from segregated Louisiana by way of inner-city California projects" born in 1934, he grew up among the constant attempts of white people to undermine his and his family's sense of dignity. But his father Charlie, his mother Katie, and his grandfather Jake each helped teach Russell to stand unyielding and strong in the face of prejudice. Russell grew up saturated with tales of resistance—not of distant leaders rallying Black people to a cause, but of his own family taking a direct stand for themselves and those they loved.

Russell's grandfather was a sharecropper in the northeast Louisiana delta. One year he informed his landlord that he would not be farming the next year. "Don't tell me what you ain't gonna do," the landlord answered. "I'll make you do it." Racial etiquette of the time dictated that Jake would acquiesce. But he did not. Instead, he replied, "Sir, you and who else?" Enraged, the landlord showed up at Jake's home that night with the Ku Klux Klan, but "The Old Man" (as Bill Russell always called him) scared them away with shotgun blasts.

Russell's father, too, contained a treasure trove of such stories. He took stands at work, at the gas station, and basically anywhere discrimination raised its head. "Mister Charlie" never seemed to blink in the face of racism's ugliness and threats. He met them with strength and unbending moral authority. Mister Charlie was Bill Russell's childhood hero, a larger-than-life exemplar of what a man could and should be.

Still, Russell's most powerful influence during those early years was probably his mother, Katie. "When I think about my mother for any reason," Russell once reflected, "what first jumps to mind are memories of her telling me that she loved me more than anyone in the world." Along with providing that bedrock of secure love and affection, Katie Russell provided yet another model of formidable dignity and self-direction. In a representative story, she once hauled Russell along after a neighbor boy had slapped him. Upon catching the bully, she instructed her son to stand up for himself and fight. Along with teaching self-respect, Katie also exhorted her son to take responsibility for his own education and intellectual development. She engaged with him in his studies, made sure he attended a good school, and regularly brought him to the library. As Russell recalled, "Every morning I felt I was going out to slay a big dragon for her and I'd come home from school to tell her how it hadn't stood a chance, just like we'd figured."

Even though the Russell family seemed more than able to handle themselves in the face of racism, in 1943 his parents tried to reduce the family's exposure to discrimination by moving from Louisiana to California. In Oakland, they hoped to find relief from the South's deeply ingrained and pervasive racism. But that hope was short-lived. At the time, Oakland's economy was booming and had drawn thousands of newcomers from across the country, many white and from the South. Whether it came west with them or not, the all-too-familiar miasma of Jim Crow racism rose in the area.

Separatist editorials began fearmongering about the violence that would erupt from mixing races. Businesses began barring Black workers from skilled positions. Renters and restaurants began refusing access to Blacks. As a result, when the Russells arrived in Oakland, they "first lived in an eight-room house shared by eight families, with another family in the garage," where "pigs, sheep, and chickens roamed the backyard." But the Russells' sense of dignity and purpose never wavered. In Charlie's decisive words, "they were broke, not poor," and "every day for four months, he stopped at the city office [for housing] to ask about his application status." Within the year, the family had moved into a racially integrated project, and the kids were attending a good school.

Then in 1946, when Russell was just twelve, a mysterious sickness took his mother's life. The bedrock of his self-confidence was suddenly gone. Even though his father remained as strong and steady a presence as ever, doing whatever it took to keep the family together and rooted in Oakland, young Bill suddenly seemed lost to himself. His humor faltered, his grades plummeted, and his young sporting career stalled. His peers mocked him to tears. "I was held back by serious doubts that I could ever become anything without my mother," he once reflected.

Amid these doubts, however, Russell still carried the memory of his mother's love and fierce ambitions for him, along with the ongoing evidence of his father's love and unflinching devotion. When aunts of the family showed up to argue that "a man can't raise two children alone," Mister Charlie refused to let the boys go. He insisted he hold to his promise to Katie, to raise the boys himself and see that they made it to college. (So serious was Katie's motherly ambition about college, she gave Russell the middle name Felton, after the president of Southern University, a historically Black university.) Regardless of how well he understood it at the time, Russell had absorbed the lessons his parents had been teaching with their words and lives. The power of their virtues was now alive in him too. As Russell put it, "respect for others, self-respect, honor, pride, dignity, commitment, loyalty, devotion, responsibility—were family traditions. So, as an adult, all I did was carry forward those traditions."

As an athlete, Russell put those principles to work, achieving two NCAA titles with the University of San Francisco (1955–56), captaincy of the gold medal-winning US Olympic basketball team (1956), five NBA MVP awards, and an outlandish eleven NBA titles with the Boston Celtics, including eight in a row and two as the country's first Black coach of a major sports team. His defending, rebounding, shot blocking, and outlet passing were praised in his day as revolutionary and innovative. Teammates, coaches, and opponents alike considered his intensity and will to win second to none.

"You can say what you want about individual players in any sport, but when it comes to winning, there is no one like Bill Russell," attested Los Angeles Lakers legend Jerry West. "I know some of those guys in other sports, like baseball and football, are great. But I don't think there ever has been anyone, in any era, who could compare to Russell . . . Really, you have to play against this man to appreciate him. Only another athlete could possibly know what I mean."

Over his 13-season career with the Boston Celtics (1956–1969), Russell played in 963 regular-season games and averaged 15.1 points, 22.5 rebounds, and 4.3 assists per game. He totaled 14,522 points, 21,620 rebounds (second-most in NBA history), and 4,100 assists. In the playoffs, his stats increased to 16.2 points and an astonishing 24.9 rebounds per game. In the NBA Finals, he played a record 70 games and grabbed 1,718 rebounds—the most in league history. He famously pulled down 40 rebounds in a Finals game on two separate occasions. And although blocked shots were not yet tracked in that era, legendary Celtics coach Red Auerbach would later estimate Russell's average at around 10 blocks per game, with another 10 forced misses from altered shots. But perhaps no statistic conveys Russell's on-court dominance better than this: he won the NBA championship in 85 percent of his seasons. (Michael Jordan's championship percentage, by comparison, is 40 percent.)

Off the court, Russell's legend shone just as brightly. He carried forward his family traditions into a habit of principled living that resulted in activism both premeditated and organic, activism that developed into a legacy. In just one of many examples, Russell led a boycott of a Celtics game in 1961, after he and other Black players were refused service at a local restaurant. "We've got to show our disapproval of this kind of treatment or else the status quo will prevail," Russell told reporters. "We have the same rights and privileges as anyone else and deserve to be treated accordingly. I hope we never have to go through this abuse again." A newspaper at the time covered the event with the headline, "Russell Would Give Up Basketball for Rights." The article notes that "Defensive genius Bill Russell said he would quit the Boston Celtics 'without hesitation' to assist the civil rights movement if it would ease racial tension . . . when asked during a news conference whether he would leave the Celts to assist in the civil rights movement, [Russell] said, "Yes, but only if it would make a concrete contribution. There'd be no choice. It would be the duty of any American."

That sort of principled and strategic thinking seemed to mark everything Russell did, from becoming the consummate champion in professional sports, to marching with civil rights leaders, or standing alongside Muhammad Ali at the Cleveland Summit. Held on June 4, 1967, the event was a pivotal gathering of prominent Black athletes—including Jim Brown, Kareem Abdul-Jabbar (then Lew Alcindor), and Russell—who met in Cleveland to discuss and ultimately support Muhammad Ali's refusal to be drafted into the Vietnam War. Their decision to stand publicly with

Ali marked a watershed moment in athlete activism, signaling a new era in which leading sports figures used their platforms to engage questions of conscience, race, and national identity. Russell's participation, alongside stars from football and boxing, underscored both the gravity of the occasion and the growing role of athletes in movements for social justice.

"We foolishly lionize athletes and make them heroes because they can hit a ball or catch one," Russell once said. "The only athletes we should bother with attaching any particular importance to are those like [Muhammad] Ali, whom we can admire for themselves and not for their incidental athletic abilities."

Russell's unbending integrity, his commitment to fairness, equality, and dignity for all, has become more than one man's inner line. It has solidified into a proverbial torch now carried and passed by professional athletes in every sport. Russell's lasting impact is summed up well by nine-time NBA champion Steve Kerr: "What he did for his country and for society and the African American community, it just dwarfs what he accomplished on the court." Given that Russell's on-court achievements were arguably the greatest ever, that is saying a lot indeed.

KAREEM
ABDUL-JABBAR
FRENCA

KAREEM ABDUL-JABBAR

After retiring from the Los Angeles Lakers in 1989, even an abbreviated list of Kareem Abdul-Jabbar's accomplishments seemed to say it all: three national championships at UCLA, three Most Outstanding Player awards at the Final Four, six NBA championships, six league MVP awards, nineteen All-Star appearances, and the NBA's all-time leading scorer (until LeBron James surpassed his record in 2023). But Abdul-Jabbar's preeminent basketball resume could not represent his ambitiousness. Not even close. His life, passion, and work had long been about far more than hoops.

At ten years old, Abdul-Jabbar (then known as Lew Alcindor) read about the murder of Emmett Till. On holiday in Mississippi from Chicago, the fourteen-year-old Till allegedly teased a white woman after buying bubblegum from her grocery store. Later that night, the woman's husband and his half-brother tracked the boy down. They invaded the home of Till's uncle, where he was staying, dragged Till outside, and beat him until unrecognizable. They then shot him, weighed him down with barbed wire, and threw his body in the Tallahatchie River. The murderers were acquitted by a jury of white men. Once legally cleared, they sold the story of their crime to *Look* magazine as a tale about "Southern justice implemented to protect white womanhood."

Learning about the incident shook Abdul-Jabbar. "It profoundly affected my sense of security in the world," he writes in *Becoming Kareem*. "Once I realized that a person, even a child, could be tortured and murdered just for being black, I no longer felt safe in my skin. . . . No one—not my parents, teachers, or friends—could explain how such a thing could happen in America."

But Till's murder also awoke something in him. "I couldn't really understand it, and it really just made me focus my mind on: 'What is this problem that causes somebody to get murdered like that?'" he once shared. "I started paying attention immediately at that moment to what was going on in the Civil Rights movement." Emmett Till's murder is often cited as the spark that ignited the civil rights movement. It certainly helped kindle a fire for change in the young Abdul-Jabbar.

During his time at Power Memorial Academy in the early 1960s, the civil rights movement steadily intensified. So did Abdul-Jabbar's desire to contribute to social justice. He began grappling with troubling questions about what fueled racism in America—racism he had suffered firsthand—and how he could help transform the country's benighted status quo.

That quest deepened at UCLA, where he was widely considered the nation's most dominant basketball player. At the end of his sophomore year in May 1967, football legend Jim Brown invited Abdul-Jabbar to meet with a group of prominent athletes and activists in Cleveland. Abdul-Jabbar accepted. At barely twenty years old, he would be the group's youngest member. Their mission? To speak with Muhammad Ali about his opposition to the military draft and the war in Vietnam. Many at the meeting hoped to change Ali's views. Some thought enlisting was his patriotic duty, others likely hoped to avoid the economic impact Ali's stance would cost the Black community. But whatever Abdul-Jabbar's thoughts entering the summit, he left inspired.

After hours of passionate discussion, Muhammad Ali's conviction remained unmoved. He refused to take part in the war. As Abdul-Jabbar recalls it, "hearing Ali's articulate defense of his moral beliefs and his willingness to suffer for them reinvigorated my own commitment to become even more politically involved." Along with that conviction, the Cleveland Summit may have given Abdul-Jabbar more insight into managing his nerves than any of the many championship games in which he played. "The stakes couldn't have been higher," he writes of the Summit, "and I felt it in my stomach the entire time I was in Cleveland. It was the longest stomachache I'd ever had."

The next year, Abdul-Jabbar began exercising his convictions with new vigor. He joined students at UCLA in demonstrating for civil rights after the assassination of Dr. Martin Luther King Jr. That peaceful act earned him a chorus of furious criticism.

Many people mischaracterized his solidarity with the cause of Dr. King as a lack of gratitude for the opportunities basketball afforded him.

Not long afterward, Abdul-Jabbar received an invitation to play basketball for the 1968 Olympic team. “I was torn,” he later wrote. “Joining the team would signal that I supported the way people of color were being treated in America—which I didn’t. Not joining the team could look like I didn’t love America—which I did.” In the end, Abdul-Jabbar decided not to play. On one hand, he did not want his presence to be co-opted as an endorsement that all was well in American society; on the other, he hoped his stance would “call attention to the rampant racial injustice of the time.” Despite the principled and measured nature of his decision, Abdul-Jabbar’s chorus of bitter critics grew in proportion to the Olympic stage. To many, especially those unfamiliar with his thoughtful, soft-spoken personality, his decision seemed standoffish or unpatriotic. But Abdul-Jabbar’s inner life had always been rich with reflection. His seeming aloofness was less detachment than discomfort with superficiality—a trait often misread by press and public alike. Nevertheless, many began calling him “un-American.”

But Abdul-Jabbar remained undeterred. His sense of integrity was clear, his commitment to social justice resolute. In keeping with his conviction, three years later in 1971, as a new NBA champion and league MVP with the Milwaukee Bucks, he publicly announced that he was now a Muslim and had changed his name from Lew Alcindor to Kareem Abdul-Jabbar (“noble servant of God”). “By changing my religion and name,” Abdul-Jabbar wrote, “I was embracing the American ideal of freedom even more than when I was Lew Alcindor. I was becoming the person I chose to be rather than the person everyone was trying to convince me I should be.” Venomous criticisms, slander, and death threats ensued. The decision to change his name and religion cost him friendships and endorsements, injured family relations, and even incited the IRS to harass him on behalf of President Richard Nixon.

Once again, however, Abdul-Jabbar stood strong. He was finally representing who he wanted to be and what he wanted to stand for. In taking these stands, he cited inspiration from observing the life of Muhammad Ali. Ali had not only sacrificed the height of his career to oppose the Vietnam War, but he had also changed his name (from Cassius Clay) to demonstrate that a person was not bound to an oppressed past or an unjust status quo. Morally speaking, any individual could choose who he or she wanted to be. “It made it easy for me as someone following in his [Ali’s] footsteps to make the choices that I made because I could see what integrity meant,”

Abdul-Jabbar said. "It might have cost him some money, but black Americans loved him and they understood where his heart was at, and it was inspiring to all of us."

That same spirit of integrity, courage, and social vision carried Kareem Abdul-Jabbar throughout the next eighteen years of his incomparable basketball career. What's more, it carried him beyond basketball, where he established himself as a best-selling author, activist, columnist, filmmaker, champion of education, and a recipient of the Presidential Medal of Freedom. As a telling example, in 2019—thirty years after retiring from the NBA—Abdul-Jabbar announced an auctioning of his personal treasures. Championship rings, famous game balls, MVP trophies, even the Herb Hess Trophy for Best Catholic Athlete of 1964—everything was up for sale. It was an unprecedented chance for collectors to own a piece of sports history.

But why the auction? Anyone surprised by Abdul-Jabbar's answer simply had not been paying attention to the man's entire life. Much of the proceeds, he announced, would go to help inspire and educate children from economically challenged schools through his Skyhook Foundation. The trove of memorabilia from his legendary athletic achievements and legacy would serve his tireless and principled pursuit of a more just, wise, and free society.

In Abdul-Jabbar's own words, representing the vision that powered his legend: "When it comes to choosing between storing a championship ring or trophy in a room, or providing kids with an opportunity to change their lives, the choice is pretty simple. Sell it all. Looking back on what I have done with my life, instead of gazing at the sparkle of jewels or gold plating celebrating something I did a long time ago, I'd rather look into the delighted face of a child holding their first caterpillar and think about what I might be doing for their future. That's a history that has no price."

FRENCH

ARTHUR ASHE

For over a century, the statues of white men who had fought for slavery and segregation loomed over Monument Avenue in Richmond, Virginia. As of 2021, however, only one figure remained along that commemorative mall in the former capital of the Confederacy: the larger-than-life likeness of the larger-than-life activist, humanitarian, and tennis legend Arthur Ashe.

Born in Richmond on July 10, 1943, Arthur Robert Ashe Jr. entered a Jim Crow culture designed to shut him out, hold him back, and keep him down. But Ashe's parents and teachers aimed to raise him strong enough to counteract that poison. As Ashe wrote in his memoir, they sought to make sure "no Black kid gave up the struggle to do better because of despair in the face of segregation. We were taught that segregation counted for nothing against our duty to ourselves to work hard and do well."

Ashe took that lesson to heart, applying himself equally to academics and athletics and excelling in both from an early age. When his father took a position that placed the family home in a Black-only 18-acre park, Ashe soon discovered the tennis courts. More importantly, it was there that seven-year-old Ashe happened upon the city's most decorated Black tennis player, Ron Charity, who was practicing his serve. After being watched for an hour, Charity stopped and decided to ask the enraptured young boy if he would like to learn to play. Ashe, of course, said he would.

Shortly after he met Charity, Ashe's mother, Mattie Cordell Cunningham Ashe, died from childbirth complications. Although Arthur Ashe Sr. worked hard to maintain a stable home for Arthur and his younger brother Johnnie, the loss of their mother created a void too vast to simply fill. Arthur "talked less and read more, and his only source of solace seemed to be the pile of books that reminded him of his mother." And there was time on the courts with Ron Charity. Turned inward by loss, Ashe poured himself into tennis. Working with Charity, Arthur developed strong tennis fundamentals, honing his form, vision, and movement. But after three years, it became clear that Ashe would need a focused coach to reach his full potential. So Charity introduced his pupil to Dr. Walter Johnson, coach of the great Althea Gibson.

Under Dr. Johnson's guidance, Ashe flourished. Despite segregation denying him access to opponents and facilities, he won many junior tournaments across the country, eventually accepting a full scholarship to UCLA. At college, Ashe more than earned his way. He became the first African American to represent the United States in the Davis Cup, won an NCAA singles title, and played a key role in UCLA claiming a national championship.

After college, when serving in the military as a data analyst at West Point, Ashe's turn toward a life of powerful activism began. It started with witnessing daily funerals for his fellow service members killed in Vietnam. The war's costs were excruciatingly clear to Ashe, while its gains were anything but. That those costs were being paid disproportionately by young Black men made the waste and injustice all the starker. Even though he was enlisted, a patriot, and a model soldier, Ashe soon became strongly opposed to military efforts in Vietnam.

Several more milestones marked 1968 as the clear launchpad for Ashe's activism. The first was a speech he delivered in March at Church of the Redeemer in Washington, DC. Although he always kept his military commitments in mind, Ashe called for Black athletes to seek transformation within their communities. He cited Jackie Robinson and Bill Russell as models that every athlete, no matter their level of accomplishment, should emulate. The speech was hardly incendiary, and yet it still won headlines that labeled him an "activist." It also provoked a warning from his military superiors not to engage publicly in that way again. The second and third milestones of 1968 came two months apart in April and June with the assassinations of Martin Luther King Jr. and Robert F. Kennedy. The loss of such civil rights leaders only galvanized Ashe's sense of duty to do as much as he could for the movement and with everything in his power. And his power increased quite a bit in August, when he reached a personal and historic milestone: Ashe became the first Black man and the lone amateur to ever win the US Open. "I'm a champion now," Ashe's brother

Johnnie recalls him saying after the victory. "People will listen to what I have to say. I'm the first Black man to win the US Open. I'm going to be sought out."

Ashe took the confidence and conviction that came with victory and, to put it mildly, he went on a run. In addition to his US Open victory, Ashe's artful, swashbuckling style of tennis carried him to another fifty titles, with highlight victories in the 1970 Australian Open and at Wimbledon in 1975. As a representative of his country, he also won five Davis Cup championships, first as a player (1968–70), then as captain (1981–82). The boy who had been barred from most courts in his hometown was now an icon starring on courts across the globe.

Ashe did not take his fame's reach for granted. As his influence deepened and broadened, his efforts to be a transformative force grew proportionally. At home in the United States, he proved to be a tireless advocate and philanthropist for civil rights, education, racial and economic equity, and the opportunity for Black and Brown children to play tennis. Ashe even led the charge for fair compensation in US tennis by helping found the Association of Tennis Professionals (ATP), which unionized and protected player interests.

As someone who considered himself a citizen of the world, Ashe increasingly turned his attention to global injustices—especially those that echoed the racial oppression he had long confronted in the United States. Among the causes he championed, none matched the focus and intensity he brought to opposing South Africa's apartheid regime. Historian Eric Allen Hall argues that Ashe developed his activist voice gradually, negotiating the tension between his role as a "racial ambassador" in predominantly white institutions and his growing obligation to challenge racial injustice wherever it appeared. Hall emphasizes that Ashe's political style was both principled and strategic: he leveraged the credibility he had earned in elite tennis circles to push for change without alienating those in power. For Hall, Ashe's activism was no less courageous for being composed. Rather, it was rooted in discipline, long-term vision, and moral clarity.

By the 1980s, Ashe had become one of the world's most visible and persistent critics of apartheid. He applied pressure on tennis officials and governments alike to isolate South Africa's government. He refused to play there under segregated conditions, spoke out in diplomatic circles, and helped lead a successful campaign to have South Africa banned from the Davis Cup. He also published widely on the issue, culminating in his 1982 book *A Hard Road to Glory*, which chronicled the history of Black athletes and argued that sports must not be detached from the fight for human rights. Ashe's moral clarity and global stature made him a rare figure: both athlete and statesman, able to shift public consensus and spur political action.

But for all his remarkable impact upon the world, it was Ashe's courage and dignity in the face of unexpected hardship that allowed him to become a symbol of hope and resolve that transcended sports, politics, and social engagement. In 1976, at the age of thirty-three, Ashe suffered a heart attack. What followed was a medical saga punctuated by quadruple coronary artery bypass surgery in 1979, reluctant retirement from tennis in 1980, a double bypass graft in 1983, and then emergency brain surgery in 1988. It was during this last surgery that doctors made a painful discovery. Ashe had HIV/AIDS. He had almost certainly contracted it during one of his heart surgeries, both of which involved significant blood transfusions, well before doctors started testing donated blood for HIV contamination.

At first, Ashe and his wife decided to keep the news private. They had just adopted a daughter and, given that AIDS was a highly stigmatized disease that frightened many, they wanted to protect their family from the turmoil the news might create. In 1992, however, *USA Today* made it known they planned to reveal Ashe's condition with a cover story. That prompted Ashe to take control of the narrative and make his own announcement. Once he did, he engaged the AIDS crisis with all his heart.

Between his announcement in April 1992 until his death from AIDS-related pneumonia on February 6, 1993, Ashe managed to change the trajectory and tone of national conversations about the disease. As usual, he rallied people and leveraged his influence to create an institution that would outlast him, the Arthur Ashe Foundation for the Defeat of AIDS, and to launch inner-city AIDS prevention programs. And simply by being himself and sharing his condition with unashamed candor, Ashe shattered the stigmas that the disease only affected drug users and homosexuals. He was a heterosexual, monogamous Black man with AIDS, and he was still the great Arthur Ashe: stylish, famous, generous, philanthropic, and a champion athlete activist. If he could conquer the malady's threat and stigma with courage and tenacity, maybe everyone could.

That same tireless will to lead by example was on display in 1992, just months before his death, when Ashe was arrested outside of the White House for protesting the US government's treatment of Haitian refugees. Despite being ill and having every excuse to be anywhere else, Ashe assured reporters that risking adversity in the cause of justice "does wonders for your outlook. I am sure it released a torrent of endorphins. Marching in a protest is a liberating experience. It's cathartic. It's one of the great moments you can have in your life."

Surveying the life of Arthur Ashe—tragically short yet miraculously rich—it is difficult to imagine there will ever be another like him. It is easy to imagine, however, his calm voice reminding us of a few powerful fundamentals: first, that each person has far more to give than just about anyone can guess; and second, that we will discover that wealth in others to the degree we learn to give of ourselves. As Ashe once put it, “From what we get, we can make a living; what we give, however, makes a life.”

NOTAH
BEGAY III
FRENCH

NOTAH BEGAY III

"To be an Indian in modern society is in a very real sense to be unreal and ahistorical," wrote Standing Rock Sioux historian and activist Vine Deloria Jr. "In so many ways, Indian people are re-examining themselves in an effort to redefine a new social structure for their people." Notah Begay III, a Diné (Navajo Nation) and Pueblo (of San Felipe and Isleta descent) professional golfer and television analyst, understands the structures of oppression that undercut Native greatness and even basic health. While the coronavirus ravaged the world, Begay pointed out that Native American reservations were "at the epicenter of this issue" due to jaw-dropping inequalities that were already firmly bricked into Indigenous existence. "It's been a scary process," he said. "I'm going to lose family members, I'm quite certain of it. And I just don't know who it's going to be." In the first years of COVID-19, Native American life expectancy plunged by a whopping six and a half years, a sharper decline than all other racial or ethnic groups in the United States. Moreover, as Begay noted, "Native American males have the shortest lifespan in America."

But Notah Begay III is a fighter. It takes more than a dash of grit and determination to win four PGA Tour titles. And Begay comes from a long family lineage of people who cut against the grain while leaning proudly on their Indigeneity. His grandfather was a Navajo code talker, serving among hundreds of Native Americans who stepped up to help the United States during World War II by speaking the Navajo language to stymie the Axis powers' efforts to intercept confidential messages. This despite the fact that the US government had brutally repressed Native speakers across the country, often sending them to boarding schools far from home under the ugly mentality prevalent among white people: "kill the Indian to save the man."

Begay did not develop his golf skills on the country-club circuit. He came up through municipal golf courses—such as the Ladera Golf Course in Albuquerque, New Mexico—serving as an all-purpose golf gopher to raise the money to afford the sport. Begay eventually made the golf squad at Stanford University, a school that, under pressure from Native students and staff in the 1970s, ditched its nickname "the Indians" and eventually replaced it with the Cardinal (the color, not the bird). Begay led Stanford to a national championship in 1994 and became a three-time All-American while earning a degree in economics. Along the way, he became teammates and close friends with golf great Tiger Woods.

Begay is not a fist-pumping political activist who takes boisterous, controversial stances in the public sphere. Instead, he is an influential barrier breaker who engages in symbolic and material actions that ripple with the political, reminding us that social representation—and showing up for people—very much matters. In 2005, he launched the Notah Begay III Foundation (NB3 Foundation) to improve Native children's health through physical activity and sports like golf and soccer. The idea is to holistically promote health and wellness to combat obesity and type 2 diabetes. American Indians and Alaska Natives die from diabetes at around twice the rate of non-Native populations. Begay noted, "Right now there are more dialysis centers being built on reservations than wellness centers." His foundation aims to change that pattern.

Begay has also been outspoken about the use of Native imagery as sports mascots. He said, "I'm 100% in support of fans cheering for their team, but cheering for your team does not mean you have to put somebody else down. It's as simple as that." Begay described Native mascots as "a very clear example of institutionalized degradation of an ethnic minority, that being the Native American people." He explained, "To classify it as simply a matter of political correctness only seeks to trivialize it a little bit, to an extent that it undermines the very human foundation of the people itself." In 2014, when evaluating the NFL's Washington franchise name and mascot ("Redskins," a dictionary-defined racial slur), he said, "I don't think if a similar racially offensive word was used for the Hispanic, African American, or Jewish communities that it would be tolerated. But because the American Indian people historically have not had much political leverage, or because we don't represent a great amount of buying power from a retail standpoint, we don't get the same level of treatment that everyone else in this country gets."

When the Washington football team finally retired its mascot in 2020, Begay said, "It made me feel good that all the work that has been put in . . . has finally come to a point that we affected change." He noted, "This was a collective effort from tribal leaders, to non-profits, to financial investment groups."

Begay summed up the mascot issue this way: "At the end of the day, my kids shouldn't have to feel bad about going to a Florida State Seminoles game or an Atlanta Braves game and watch somebody run around who is not respecting the origins of who we are as Indian people. I love to cheer for my team, but in order to cheer for my team I shouldn't have to belittle or disrespect somebody else's existence."

The representation of Native people is no trivial matter. Research finds that Native mascots are psychologically detrimental to Indigenous students, decreasing their self-esteem. Such mascots also undermine racial relations and foment racism. When white people are exposed to Native American mascots, they tend to show heightened prejudice toward Indigenous peoples and less support for Native sovereignty.

Begay eschews the activist label, opting instead for humanistic influence. "I'm an advocate—an advocate of positive American Indian issues. I just want to break down stereotypes and educate people." He is a barrier breaker who is willing to stand up for justice in public.

Begay has his eye on the big picture. "When I look back," he said, "and I'm taking my last breaths, I won't be thinking about golf scores and trophies. I'll be looking at the generation behind me and whether I was an inspiration to them to improve their lives." He said, "We don't know our potential unless we run as hard as we can as fast as we can toward it. I don't know the impact I can make because I don't want to predetermine what those outcomes should be or could be. I just want to work as hard as I can every year, serve as many kids as I can." Therefore, he has chosen "to commit to a life of service for as long as I can."

SERENA
WILLIAMS
FRENCH

SERENA WILLIAMS

"If you're a girl from Compton, become the greatest athlete ever," Colin Kaepernick said of Serena Williams in his popular Nike ad that implored us to "Believe in something, even if it means sacrificing everything." Williams, the African American tennis icon, certainly believed in herself en route to winning twenty-three Grand Slam titles, four Olympic gold medals, and holding the number one slot in the singles rankings for a whopping 319 weeks. But it didn't mean she had to sacrifice *everything*. Williams somehow managed to do it all.

In our introduction to this book, we noted that athlete activism tends to arrive in two main shapes: 1) direct engagement with politics and 2) symbolic actions that often take the form of social representation rather than premeditated political undertakings. Through both her actions and her identity, Serena Williams explodes that dichotomy. She has spoken out forcefully against racism in tennis and wider society while, as an African American on the majority-white tennis circuit, has served as a formidable role model.

In some ways, Williams's entire career can be understood as subversive. As scholar Lori Latrice Martin put it, "Serena's body type and power-filled performances do not necessarily conform to expectations in the sports world for women athletes, but they especially do not conform to expectations in tennis, which has not historically been considered a power sport and where few Black women, until recently, have played in substantial numbers and with such great success." While standing on the shoulders of African American tennis greats like Althea Gibson and Ora Washington, Serena Williams pushed back against the white, upper-class tennis establishment with the same verve as her blistering serve. As a high-profile, high-performing athlete, she used her platform to facilitate change inside and outside the sport.

Much of Serena's early activism and advocacy is rooted in family. Richard Williams and Oracene Price trained, prepared, and fortified their daughters—not only Serena but also her older sister Venus, a seven-time Grand Slam singles champion—as they emerged on the tennis scene. The Williams family forged their own path through the sport, training on the dilapidated courts of Compton, California, as they sharpened their game. By the mid-1990s, the sisters had emerged as phenoms on the junior tennis circuit. Williams and Price instilled in the girls a deep sense of pride and a commitment to protect each other while also cultivating media literacy and an ability to advocate for themselves and others. These early parental lessons shaped the way Serena and Venus handled themselves on and off the court.

Being a young Black star in the tennis world was no walk in the racialized park. In March 2001, Serena Williams was slated to face her sister Venus in the semifinals of the Indian Wells tournament in California. When Venus chose to default just before the match, thereby allowing Serena to advance in the tournament, racial epithets and boisterous booing rained down on Venus and their father Richard Williams. Some media accounts actually blamed the Williams trio, and especially the father, for injecting race into tennis. Meanwhile, tennis star Martina Hingis, a former number one player in the world, downplayed their racist treatment, claiming that the Williams sisters only benefited from being African American, that "They have had a lot of advantages because they can always say, 'It's racism.'" Because of their experience at Indian Wells, Serena Williams boycotted the tournament for fourteen years. In an essay she penned for *Time* magazine announcing her return, she said that the racist experience in 2001 "haunted me for a long time. It haunted Venus and our family as well." She added, "I play for the love of the game. And it is with that love in mind, and a new understanding of the true meaning of forgiveness, that I will proudly return to Indian Wells in 2015." Williams made it clear that she was in charge of her own narrative.

As Serena's individual star power rose, she used her position to continue to advocate for change both on and off the tennis court. She supported her sister Venus in her successful quest to persuade the tennis brass at Wimbledon's All England Club to award women tennis players the same prize money as their male counterparts. The sisters also teamed up to found a resource center for victims of violence in their hometown of Compton, naming it after their elder sister Yetunde Price, who was murdered in a gang-related drive-by shooting in 2003.

Serena refused to conform to the conservative sartorial standards maintained by the white power structure overseeing the sport. Her outfits—including a glorious form-hugging bodysuit that she first unveiled at the 2018 French Open—set trends in Black style, pushed the boundaries of sportswear, and sent stodgy tennis honchos into a frenzy. The French Tennis Federation president stated that Williams's full-length bodysuit would not be allowed in the future, even though the garment was designed to reduce the possibility of blood clots, something Williams was especially susceptible to after the birth of her daughter the previous year. Her wholly practical yet boldfaced style choices called attention to the policing of women's bodies in sport. Moreover, Jaime Schultz has argued that the very term "catsuit"—often used by journalists and others to describe Williams's clothing style—was racist and sexist, making space to comment on the tennis player's muscularity, often in pejorative terms. "It is impossible to disarticulate the representations of Serena Williams's blackness from consideration of her gendered, classed, and sexualized subjectivities—each one compounds the others," she wrote.

Williams's challenges to the status quo have resulted in policy changes. After giving birth to her daughter Olympia in 2017, Williams nearly died from complications involving a pulmonary embolism, a condition whereby blood clots block one or more arteries in the lungs. She turned her harrowing experience into action, publicly trumpeting the jaw-dropping racial disparities around maternal health: African American women are three times as likely to die from giving birth, while globally, access to safe birthing spaces varies significantly by race and class. In an essay she wrote for CNN, Williams advocated for action: "You can demand governments, businesses and health care providers do more to save these precious lives."

The realization that she had won the Australian Open while pregnant was heralded by many as continued proof of how amazing women's bodies are. However, it was Williams's return to the tennis court after giving birth that made socio-political waves. Once she rejoined the professional tennis circuit, she was unranked, as returning from a pregnancy was treated like returning from an injury. Williams saw the injustice in this and prompted a debate about how maternity leave should be treated by the Women's Tennis Association. This led to a 2019 rule change that introduced a special ranking system designed to avoid penalizing women who were returning from childbirth.

As Williams has stepped away from actively competing in tennis she established her own fashion line: S by Serena. She also founded Serena Ventures, a venture-capital company, after learning that less than two percent of all venture-capital funds went to women. For Serena, a corporate approach to activism has emerged. As of 2024 nearly 80 percent of the company's portfolio is invested in underrepresented founders, over half of which are women-led companies and nearly half are owned by Black founders.

Serena is also using corporate investment to increase opportunity, visibility, and investment in women's sports. "Tennis has had its moments and it is international and it is huge and it's always going to be there," Serena explained, "It is time to lift up other sports, women's soccer, women's basketball like there are so many other sports that have been doing so great. Let's put them on a platform that tennis is on." Williams has already invested in women's soccer as a founding owner of Angel City FC in the National Women's Soccer League. In 2025, she also purchased a share of the WNBA's Toronto Tempo.

While corporate activism has its limitations, it is clear that by using her platform and capital to open doors for others and disrupt the status quo Serena has been an effective agent of change. After investing $1.3 million into a women's sports initiative in partnership with Nike, Williams said she hopes to amplify the voices of other women athletes and to convert insights into actions in the wider battle for gender equality.

Serena Williams bid farewell to tennis in August 2022. In an essay for *Vogue*, she announced the end of her competitive career, although she preferred the word "evolution" to retirement. She wrote, "I'd like to think that thanks to opportunities afforded to me, women athletes feel that they can be themselves on the court." She added, "They can play with aggression and pump their fists. They can be strong yet beautiful. They can wear what they want and say what they want and kick butt and be proud of it all." Her impact on the game of tennis is undeniable. On and off the court, Serena has blazed a trail and remained staunchly committed to fighting for racial justice and gender equality. Whatever Serena Williams does next in this world will surely be an electrifying, deliberate chapter in the life of one of the most influential athletes of the twenty-first century.

JAMES
EBR
ON
FRENCH

LEBRON JAMES

The nickname came early: "King James." Sportswriters started using it while LeBron James was still in high school—part prophecy, part branding. It stuck not because he asked for it, but because it fit. On the court, James didn't just dominate. He inspired onlookers with a sense that there was something about him—something commanding, something inevitable.

But the air of inevitability people sensed was hard-earned. Before the nickname fit and greatness seemed a foregone conclusion, LeBron James had to fight through uncertainty, instability, and a world that offered him no guarantees. Born on December 30, 1984, to a sixteen-year-old single mother in Akron, Ohio, James spent his early years the way many underprivileged kids do: moving from couch to couch, living from meal to meal, drifting in and out of school, hungering for structure, hunting for hope. Through trials and tribulations, he learned tenacity. Through his mother Gloria's care, he learned to believe others could care too. Young LeBron James may have faced hardship and isolation, but from them he wrested the core lessons of character and community that would establish him as an NBA all-time great, a global icon, a powerful businessman, and an intrepid philanthropist who would always remember his roots. In short, he was learning how to become King James.

The stage was set. James's potential simply needed to rendezvous with the right opportunity. That opportunity arrived when Bruce Kelker drove by the parking lot of the housing complex where James and his mother were staying with friends. Kelker was coach of the East Dragons, a rec-league football team for boys under 10. He noticed a group of boys playing tag and approached them with a talent scout's mentality. Whoever won a footrace across the parking lot, he promised, would become the East Dragons' running back. Eight-year-old LeBron James won by fifteen yards.

In a way, James never looked back from that victorious race. Through connections with Kelker and the East Dragons, in the fall of 1993, LeBron found what would become a formative experience of family. Frank and Pam Walker, parents of Frankie Walker Jr., one of James's teammates, invited him to stay with them. The arrangement would allow James to live with them in their suburban Akron home, to enjoy continuity with school, and to still see his mother on weekends. Not only did this arrangement give James a chance to stay with his football team, it also allowed him to experience what a family could build together with stability, vision, discipline, and resources.

The new situation also introduced James to basketball. The Walkers had a hoop mounted on their garage in the backyard, over a dirt court. There, Mr. Walker taught the boys the fundamentals of the game, skills like dribbling and offhand layups. One lesson Mr. Walker did not have to teach James, however, was how to be teachable. James would always take to heart the lessons Walker taught. He would listen, apply, and grow. Thanks to his receptive attitude, James improved every time he practiced. That gift, according to Frank Walker—of all James's herculean gifts—was and is his greatest. "If you teach him something," says Walker, "he'll apply it to his game."

Ten years later, LeBron had used that gift to grow his way into the first pick of the 2003 NBA draft. After leading St. Vincent–St. Mary High School in Akron to three state championships, the Cleveland Cavaliers drafted the Ohio-grown legend with the first pick in the 2003 NBA draft. For the league, it turned out to be a watershed moment. The anticipation surrounding James was unprecedented, and he did not disappoint. James quickly became the definitive NBA player of his era. He won championships and MVP awards and led his teams to eight straight league Finals—all while becoming the NBA's all-time leading scorer, eclipsing Kareem Abdul-Jabbar's record in 2023—and amassing stats that approached historic triple-double averages. James even became the first in NBA history to play alongside his son in an NBA game. His accomplishments have ensured, at the very least, that any serious debate about the greatest player of all time will now have to consider the magisterial legacy of LeBron James.

And yet James's historic impact upon basketball may still be overshadowed by his influence upon culture and society. To the NBA, James has been a juggernaut, a phenomenon, a King; to the world, he has been something even more. Fans may argue endlessly about where he ranks on the basketball court as an all-time great, but where he ranks off it is incomparable: James is his own thing, the first of his kind, the active heir not simply of basketball as a game, but of basketball as a cultural force and a global business.

The right player at the right time, James is the beneficiary of the NBA's successful run through the 1980s and 1990s, inheriting an immense wealth of cultural capital earned by marketable greats like Magic Johnson, Larry Bird, and, of course, Michael Jordan. This inheritance, combined with James's acumen and ambition, has empowered him to become what sportswriter Dave Zirin calls "that rarest of commodities: the activist mogul." Most professional athletes, in other words, remain *under* their sport, citizens of their league. The games can go on without them. The business that the games generate can too. Most athletes are dispensable in that way. James, by contrast, managed to become the NBA's avatar, both superstar and institution—an individual athlete with his own unique story, and yet at the same time, a living symbol tasked with representing the present and past ethos of a diverse, dynamic, and socially engaged league.

Not only has James proven himself a master student of the on-court skills that came before him, he also dedicated himself to carrying the torch of the league's rich activist tradition. As Jerry Bembry notes, whether "from wearing hoodies with his Miami Heat teammates in 2012 to protest the shooting of Trayvon Martin to wearing 'I Can't Breathe' T-shirts in 2014 in a tribute to the killing of Eric Garner (who shouted those words while dying in a police chokehold) to his criticism of President Donald Trump," James has consistently lent his name and raised his voice for social justice. Although he drew criticism early in his career for staying silent on political issues, James emerged in the 2010s as one of the most creative athlete activists of his generation.

Following the same philosophy he uses in business—pursuing ownership of whatever he helps produce and popularize—James has invested in the power of media to promote justice and cultural change through many voices and lenses, not just his own. Through SpringHill Company, James has championed underrepresented voices in media, producing films that tackle themes like NCAA exploitation (*Student Athlete*), political resistance in sports (*Shut Up & Dribble*, *What's My Name: Muhammad Ali*, and *Jim Thorpe: Lit By Lightning*), and the multifaceted lives of athletes off the court (*More Than an Athlete*). His push for ownership—acquiring stakes in Liverpool F.C., Blaze Pizza, and even a production company—further reflects a new model of athlete empowerment.

Perhaps James's most impactful contribution is the I Promise School, opened in 2018 in Akron, which offers free tuition, meals, bikes, college scholarships, and wraparound services for at-risk youth and their families. It is a living embodiment of James's belief in education, opportunity, and staying connected to one's roots. At the founding of the school, James made clear what the project meant to him: "This is a huge moment not only in my life, in my family's life and the foundation's life, but in these kids' lives as well. . . . As a kid from Akron, I remember walking these same streets. When people ask me why a school, that's the reason why. I know what these kids are going through. I know their dreams. I know their nightmares. I know what they're going through. That's why this school is here." According to James, none of his championships or MVP awards compare to his sense of accomplishment in establishing the I Promise School.

Few twenty-first-century professional athletes engage in activism as consistently and purposefully as James, and fewer still do so while bearing the status of a global icon. His influence depends on the very infrastructure activism often seeks to challenge: corporate wealth, public consensus, and the risk-averse management of a global brand. And yet James has tried to inhabit both worlds at once—to be both institution and outsider, establishment and resistance. That ambition has expanded what athlete activism can look like. It has also produced moments of tension.

In 2019, for example, after Houston Rockets General Manager Daryl Morey tweeted support for Hong Kong protesters, James criticized the timing of the message, warning it could cause harm "financially . . . physically, emotionally, spiritually." He later clarified that his remarks weren't about the protests themselves but about the responsibilities of using social media. Still, backlash was swift. Critics accused James of prioritizing business interests over principle—especially given his vocal stance on domestic political issues. He defended his intent but ultimately stepped back from the controversy. The criticism faded, and his reputation endured.

The incident did highlight, however, the immense challenge of representing a global brand *and* serving as an activist icon. But LeBron James has never been one to shy away from a challenge. Likewise, he has never been one to fit regular molds. He has built his career upon obliterating expectations for roles others insist are already defined. What is a point guard? What is a power forward? What is a superstar? What is an activist? James has his own ideas. And as his story teaches, in the long run, his ideas usually offer something revolutionary.

MEGAN
RAPINOE
FRENCH

MEGAN RAPINOE

When Megan Rapinoe collected the player of the year trophy at FIFA's annual gala award ceremony in September 2019, her acceptance speech fizzed with the political. She implored the soccer megastars in the audience to "lend your platform to other people, lift other people up, share your success. We have a unique opportunity in football different to any other sport in the world to use this beautiful game to actually change the world for better . . . Do something, do anything. We have incredible power in this room."

That day Rapinoe followed her own advice to "lift other people up." She honored Sahar Khodayari, the feminist activist who courageously challenged Iran's ban on women in sports stadiums before dying by self-immolation. She highlighted the anti-racism work being done by Raheem Sterling and Kalidou Koulibaly, two Black footballers in Europe who endured racist abuse from spectators. She praised women footballers ensconced in the battle for equal pay. And she boosted LGBTQ athletes, mentioning Collin Martin, the only out gay player in US men's professional soccer at the time.

In accepting the award, Rapinoe catapulted an additional key point into conversation: solidarity is vital. For her, it's imperative that white athletes stand with athletes of color, that straight athletes link arms in struggles with LGBTQ athletes, that male soccer players support women's fight for equal pay. Acknowledging different forms of privilege, and acting from that base of understanding, is key.

Rapinoe walks the walk. She is one of the few white athletes to take a knee to make a stand with NFL star Colin Kaepernick in his public challenge to the racialized criminal legal system and disproportionate police violence against people of color in the United States. Rapinoe reasoned, "Those who are discriminated against shouldn't have to fight alone, and leaving advocacy to the marginalized group itself—the group most at risk of dismissal or reprisal—is, frankly, outrageous." She also asserted, "It's important to have white people stand in support of people of color on this. We don't need to be the leading voice, of course, but standing in support of them is something that's really powerful." Rapinoe then connected the intersectional dots: "Being a gay American, I know what it means to look at the flag and not have it protect all of your liberties."

In response to Rapinoe's decision to take a knee, the US Soccer Federation passed a policy that was clearly designed to squelch her dissent and to dissuade others from taking action. It mandated that players "shall stand respectfully during the playing of national anthems." Rapinoe obeyed the letter of the rule—even while deeming it "backwards"—but with a dissident twist. She said, "I'll probably never put my hand over my heart," adding, "I'll probably never sing the national anthem again."

Ahead of the 2019 World Cup in France, she hit her activist stride, and she wasn't afraid to take it straight at President Donald Trump. In one interview she called him "sexist," "misogynistic," "small-minded," "racist," and "not a good person." Rapinoe managed to wrangle the president's attention when video emerged in which she vowed that if the United States won the World Cup, "I'm not going to the fucking White House."

Trump's Twitter thumbs sprang into action. In a string of tweets he berated Rapinoe, if in somewhat passive-aggressive fashion: "I am a big fan of the American Team, and Women's Soccer, but Megan should WIN first before she TALKS! Finish the job!. Megan should never disrespect our Country, the White House, or our Flag, especially since so much has been done for her & the team. Be proud of the Flag that you wear. The USA is doing GREAT!"

"Finish the job" she did, notching two goals in the next match and another in the final on the way to winning both the Golden Boot (the award for top goal scorer of the tournament) and the Golden Ball (the award for top player). She said, "I stand by the comments that I made about not wanting to go to the White House with exception of the expletive." She added, "My mom will be very upset about that."

All the while, Rapinoe has continued to speak out on hot-button social issues, whether it be wealth inequality and homelessness or mass incarceration and police brutality. Such issues are no mere abstraction: her older brother Brian has struggled with addiction, his adult life a revolving door in and out of the prison system.

Rapinoe has also been a vibrant voice in the fight for equal pay for women athletes. In 2016, she and four other US Women's National Team (USWNT) stars—Carli Lloyd, Alex Morgan, Becky Sauerbrunn, and Hope Solo—lodged a wage discrimination complaint with the Equal Employment Opportunity Commission. Then, in March 2019, just ahead of the World Cup, she joined twenty-seven USWNT players in a gender-discrimination lawsuit against the US Soccer Federation. In claiming wage discrimination, the plaintiffs argued that US Soccer paid members of the men's team far more, despite the women eclipsing the men's success. When Rapinoe and her US teammates victoriously hoisted the World Cup trophy in France, fans spontaneously chanted "Equal pay! Equal pay!" In 2022, the US Soccer Federation became the sport's first national governing body to sign agreements promising equal compensation for its men's and women's teams.

Rapinoe came out publicly as gay in 2012. She has worked doggedly to create space for others to express their sexuality and to be their true selves. She was the first publicly gay athlete to appear in the *Sports Illustrated* swimsuit edition. She and her then-partner, basketball superstar Sue Bird, appeared together as the first gay couple in *ESPN the Magazine*'s Body Issue. After the United States edged France 2–1 in a quarterfinal match at the 2019 World Cup, with Rapinoe notching both US goals, she was asked how it felt to be so successful during Pride Month. She chirped "Go gays!" before quipping, "You can't win a championship without gays on your team—it's never been done before, ever. That's science, right there!"

When Rapinoe retired from soccer in 2023, she made it clear that she felt her off-field activism was as important as her on-field accolades. "I think we've been a big part of pushing, talking about whether it's gay rights or racial justice or trans rights, more into every conversation around sports, in particular around women's sports," she said of the work she and her teammates had done, adding, "We've been such a driver of that and have made that just as important as what we are doing on the field."

Through her athlete activism, Rapinoe both transcends sport while honing a fighting spirit that is grounded in political movements that are firmly tethered to earth. "I feel like I'm a walking protest," she once said. And the world is better for it.

TORCHBEARERS

REIMAGINE

Torchbearers have accepted the broad mantle of activism and expanded it, bringing faith, culture, gender, mental health, and collective care further into the tradition.

MOORE

MAYA MOORE

In 2018, a new billboard went up in downtown Minneapolis that featured a giant black-and-white image of Minnesota Lynx star Maya Moore with her arms outstretched, a recreation of Michael Jordan's iconic 1989 "Wings" poster. Moore was the first women's basketball player signed to the Jordan brand. Like Jordan's poster, the powerful billboard included a quote from the poet William Blake. Under Moore's arms, the modified quote read: *No bird soars too high, if she soars with her own wings.*

Maya Moore used her own wings to soar to new heights on and off the court. In basketball, she was an undeniable champion. From an early age the spotlight was bright and the expectations were high. Moore was named the National Gatorade Player of the Year in high school and was already turning heads on the court. In college she continued show-stopping and dominant performances, ultimately leading the University of Connecticut to two national titles, including an undefeated season. It was no surprise when Moore was the number one pick in the 2011 WNBA draft.

Moore quickly became one of the stars of the WNBA. "Having Maya shook the league and made people pay attention to us," said Monica Wright, who played with Moore on the Minnesota Lynx. Moore had entered the WNBA in its fifteenth season. New television deals, brand sponsorships, and superstars like Moore helped elevate the growing league. "We have an incredible product in the WNBA," said Moore after joining the league. "It's amazing when you come in person and see how powerful and strong and fast the women's game is. It's beautiful and exciting, with the energy of a college game and the quality of world-class pros."

As a rookie in 2011, Moore helped the Lynx win the championship, earning Rookie of the Year honors along the way. The sky-high expectations for Moore grew even higher. Over the next six years, Moore would become one of the faces of a basketball dynasty as the Lynx won the WNBA championship again in 2013, 2015, and 2017. As a face of the league, Moore remained outspoken about growing the game on the players' terms. She argued that visibility and investment were key to the future of the league and used her platform as a Jordan brand ambassador to develop camps, clinics, and pipelines for girls in basketball. Moore refused to sacrifice the integrity of the WNBA, saying, "I don't want to compromise our identity as basketball players to become something that we think people will like on a superficial level. Celebrate us for the things that matter."

Maya Moore believed that it was important for athletes to make the most of their public platforms. Moore saw community engagement, leadership, and social activism as league-wide traits, and for her, all this only strengthened the platform she stood on. "When you know the women on the court stand for things worth believing in, you'll take your kids and then they will take theirs," Moore argued in 2015. Just one year later, Moore would take her biggest stand yet as she led the new wave of athletic resistance in protest of police brutality.

In 2016, following the shooting deaths of Alton Sterling, Philando Castile, and Dallas police officers, Moore and her three co-captains, Seimone Augustus, Rebekkah Brunson, and Lindsay Whalen, showed up to a press conference wearing shirts that read "Change Starts with Us: Justice and Accountability." On the back of the shirt, underneath Sterling's and Castile's names and a Dallas Police insignia, was the phrase *Black Lives Matter*. At the press conference, Moore spoke about why they felt the need to take action. "We as a nation can decide to stand up for what is right, no matter your race, background or social status," Moore told reporters. "It is time that we take a deep look at our ability to be compassionate and empathetic to those suffering from the problems that are deep within our society. Again, this is a human issue, and we need to speak out for change together."

In the weeks following the Lynx's action, NBA players would speak out about racial injustice at the ESPY Awards, and WNBA players around the league would protest by wearing black shirts. Soon basketball players in the pros and in college were wearing "I Can't Breathe" shirts, converting the last words of Eric Garner, a victim of police brutality in New York, into a rallying call for action. Initially, the WNBA was hesitant to support its players' activism. Indeed, the league initially fined Moore and her teammates, along with the Phoenix Mercury and the New York

Liberty, for their protest actions. But Moore and her fellow WNBA players refused to back down.

The persistence on the part of athletes like Moore shaped the WNBA's future. League executives finally conceded that Moore was right: standing for something could be celebrated and infused the WNBA with an activist identity. By 2018, the WNBA launched the "Take a Seat, Take a Stand" initiative that marketed the league as community-oriented and politically engaged. Each ticket sale doubled as a donation to one of the league's identified organizations or causes.

It would also be the last season Moore formally played in the WNBA.

In February 2019, Maya Moore made a shocking announcement: she was taking the season off. In a written piece for *The Players' Tribune,* Moore explained that her faith called on her to "shift focus" onto other things for the moment. In particular, she felt called to work on prison reform that she had been introduced to via her family's prison ministry. "I get pretty worked up when I see injustice and I couldn't pretend like I didn't see this happening," Moore had previously been vocal about her work in prisons. Specifically, her time away allowed her to focus her efforts on the Jonathan Irons case.

In 1998, 16-year-old Jonathan Irons was found guilty of burglary and assault with a deadly weapon. He was sentenced to 50 years in jail. When Moore became involved, Irons had been behind bars for over 20 years. Noting many suspicious issues with the case, Moore began working to prove that Irons had been wrongly convicted. She highlighted glaring issues in both the case and the larger criminal justice system. "Athletes are speaking with increasing urgency about social issues, but few are as engaged as Moore," observed Kurt Streeter at *The New York Times*. "Convinced that Irons has been victimized by a racist justice system, she has given money and time toward a last gasp bid for his release."

The dedication and conviction Moore exhibited by stepping away from the game underscored her belief that the athlete activist could play an important role in the pursuit of social justice. "We have so much influence in our culture," Moore explained, "we feel so moved and want to use a voice to try to speak to justice and human issues."

The decision to sit out the season also placed Moore in a smaller group of activist athletes: those who sacrificed their athletic careers to stand up for their convictions. Renowned sports sociologist and architect of the Olympic Project for Human Rights, Dr. Harry Edwards, likened Moore to Muhammad Ali, Colin Kaepernick, and Curt Flood. "What Ali gave up made the magnitude of his commitment even greater. What Curt Flood gave up made the magnitude of that commitment even greater.

Because not only were they doing it on principle . . . but they walked away from so much to do it."

Measured in dollars and cents, the magnitude of what Ali, Kaepernick, and Flood walked away from was far greater than the WNBA salary that Moore left behind. However, that simple equation elides the depth of Moore's sacrifice. As the face of an ever-growing league, one that had been hoisted onto her shoulders, the decision to walk away potentially jeopardized the continued evolution of the WNBA. Certainly, Moore faced some criticism for her decision based on this fear. Yet it would soon become clear that Moore had left the WNBA a blueprint, an ethos of activism, and an articulation about how they might use their platform for justice.

In January 2020, the WNBA Player's Association announced that they had reached a new agreement with the league in the most comprehensive collective bargaining agreement seen in women's basketball at that time. A week later, Moore once again announced she was sitting out the upcoming season *and* the 2020 Summer Olympics to continue her work on Irons's case and prison reform.

Then coronavirus came.

By spring 2020, the Olympics had been postponed, the WNBA season was in jeopardy, and the entire world had shut down due to COVID-19. Eventually it was decided that the WNBA would hold a season in the "Wubble" ("women" + "bubble"), created at IMG Academy in Bradenton, Florida. The complex featured a single-site court and space where teams would all live, eat, and play together over the course of the summer. Yet as players prepared to enter the Wubble, a video of George Floyd being murdered by police officers in Minneapolis went viral. Breonna Taylor's police-shooting case in Louisville resurfaced, and Ahmaud Arbery was shot and killed by two white men while jogging in Satilla Shores, Georgia.

These viral snapshots of Black death and racist violence reignited a wave of grassroots protest, including athletic activism. Once again, WNBA players committed to using their platform for change. The league dedicated its season to the #SayHerName movement, specifically highlighting Black girls and women who had been victims of state-sanctioned violence. They wore shirts, wrote slogans on the court, and used breaks in the games to recognize and promote the families and stories of girls and women like Sandra Bland, Breonna Taylor, and Aiyana Stanley-Jones.

There were also players who refused to play. Natasha Cloud, Tiffany Hayes, and Renee Montgomery announced they were sitting out of the season to focus their efforts on social justice. It was clear that Maya Moore was their blueprint. "I always make sure to tell people she's a trailblazer," Montgomery said of Moore. "Everybody gets why I do it now. She did it two years ago. I'm getting a lot of media attention for what I'm doing; they did it before it was cool, before it was understood." That summer, as WNBA players advocated for change both on and off the court, Maya Moore watched Jonathan Irons walk free. The work that she and others had done on Irons's case had paid off, and in July 2020, his conviction was overturned.

The activism of women athletes is often overlooked. The actions Moore and her teammates took in 2016 were less visible than those of the NBA players on the ESPY stage or Colin Kaepernick kneeling for the anthem in the weeks following. The resurgence of activism in the summer of 2020 was a reminder that the WNBA had a long history of activism and social justice. When other leagues scrambled to set up social-justice councils and respond to the political moment, they looked to the WNBA for guidance. And the WNBA continued to lead.

When Kelly Loeffler, a part-owner of the Atlanta Dream, fueled her US Senate reelection bid by publicly admonishing WNBA activism and calling #BlackLivesMatter divisive, WNBA players took action. Refusing to be political pawns in Loeffler's brazen campaign, players on the Dream instead researched and met with her electoral opponents. They eventually decided to endorse Reverend Raphael Warnock in the Georgia Senate race. WNBA players donned #VoteWarnock shirts, canvassed throughout Georgia, staged voter registration drives, and partnered with existing grassroots organizers in the state. Warnock won the Senate race and helped flip Georgia blue, even influencing the 2020 presidential election. The Warnock campaign credited the WNBA for boosting his campaign at a critical time.

For WNBA players, Maya Moore remains a legend. On the court she was a phenom: a player they wanted to learn from, to emulate, to try to beat. Off the court she carried the league on her back and pushed the WNBA to new marketing deals and visibility. She also modeled conviction, stood bravely on her platform, and used it to do the work to build a better world. In 2023, Maya Moore was a first-ballot selection for the Women's Basketball Hall of Fame. In 2025, she was chosen for induction into the Naismith Basketball Hall of Fame. Her legacy, on and off the court, is evident in the continued trajectory and justice commitments of the league. Just like her Minneapolis billboard predicted, Maya Moore soared to new heights. For a whole generation of athletes, activists, and fans alike, she has played and advocated and lived in a way that has everyone saying: Be Like Maya.

CHRIS
MOSiER

CHRIS MOSIER

When the US House of Representatives passed the Equality Act in February 2021, it meant to extend discrimination protections for sex and gender identity to safeguard LGBTQ people in matters of employment, housing, education, and "public accommodations" like sports stadiums, transportation providers, and retail stores. The legislation built from the US Supreme Court's decision in June 2020 that the 1964 Civil Rights Act provisions on "sex" applied to lesbian, gay, bisexual, and transgender people in the US. Since then, the US has experienced a sharp political backlash.

All too often, the T in LGBTQ is left out of the political discussion. Transgender athlete Chris Mosier is fighting to fix that omission. Mosier is a world-class triathlete, and in 2015 he became the first transgender man to represent the United States in international competition. He is a six-time member of Team USA in duathlon and triathlon, and in 2019 he was a two-time national champion in race walking. The following year he competed in the 50-kilometer race walk at the US Olympic Trials. Mosier was also the first transgender athlete to be featured in the ESPN Body Issue. In short, he is an athlete who has reached the pinnacle of elite athletics while simultaneously blazing a trail for trans people everywhere. "I love breaking barriers," he said. "I love making a clearer pathway for the people who come after me."

Mosier's success followed a female-to-male transition that began in 2010 when he changed his legal documentation to male and began a regimen of testosterone injections. Yet his road began earlier: when he was four years old, he was already grappling with gender identity. In high school he presented himself in androgynous fashion, which elicited flak from his classmates. He described how the pushback he receives as a transgender athlete today is significantly less intense than the tension he experienced for years as a female athlete who self-identified as male.

Mosier is committed to demystifying all things trans. To that end, he has created the website www.transathlete.com, which defines transgender—or trans—this way: "A term describing a person's gender identity that does not necessarily match their assigned sex at birth. Transgender people may or may not decide to alter their bodies hormonally and/or surgically to match their gender identity." Mosier notes that transgender is also a general term for those "who transcend conventional expectations of gender identity or expression—such groups include, but are not limited to, people who identify as transsexual, genderqueer, gender variant, gender diverse, and androgynous." Trans athletes have also become influential in the sports world.

Prominent transgender individuals have helped place trans issues into the mainstream, with celebrities like Laverne Cox, Elliot Page, and Chaz Bono raising awareness. The sports world features trans folks as well. Renée Richards played professional tennis in the late 1970s and early 1980s. There's also Caitlyn Jenner—the gold-medal-winning Olympian from the 1976 Games—and Kye Allums, who in 2010 became the first known trans man to play college women's basketball for George Washington University. The 2020 Summer Olympics in Tokyo featured numerous trans athletes, including non-binary US skateboarder Alana Smith, gold-medal-winning non-binary Canadian soccer player Quinn, and New Zealand's Laurel Hubbard, who competed in weightlifting. In 2022, Lia Thomas, a swimmer at the University of Pennsylvania, became the first transgender athlete to win a title in NCAA Division I sports, claiming victory in the 500-yard freestyle. Quinn also participated at the 2024 Olympics in Paris, while non-binary runner Nikki Hiltz represented the United States in the 800-meter competition.

The terrain of sports has not only emerged as a key space to expand transgender visibility, but also as a principal battleground over the rights of transgender people. Under President Donald Trump, the anti-trans backlash has been intense. In the first two months of his second term, he signed twelve anti-trans executive orders, including one titled "Keeping Men Out of Women's Sports." With the support of conservative think tanks, state legislators are emboldened: the first half of 2025 saw more than 940 anti-trans bills introduced across the US. Often, language in the bills is suspiciously similar, pointing to a coordinated effort.

Mosier has been unwavering in his fight against such legislation, energetically challenging the political forces that are trying to further marginalize trans people and erase their existence. He views these bills as a confected "wedge issue" designed to "divide voter bases" and "gain traction for conservative politicians" even though the efforts are "not rooted in fact or science." Mosier noted, "Some of these organizations focus specifically on keeping athletes out of sport, and that's their entry point into trying to erase trans people from public life." All this, he said, was part of "a clear underlying effort to actively discriminate and harass trans people."

For Mosier, trans participation in sport is a straightforward social-justice issue. "When we're talking about young people in sports, we should not be using the same standards as we're using at the most elite level of sports," he said. More generally, "Trans women are women and trans girls are girls, and they belong in girls' and women's sports." All too often "people are negating and erasing the identity of the trans person, not actually taking into consideration what it means to be transgender. There are not men pretending to be women to get ahead in women's sports. It's just not happening." He added, "We know that there are many very real problems in gender equity in sports, but trans athletes are not one of them."

Mosier's advocacy has won results. He challenged the International Olympic Committee to adjust its rules around transgender participation at the Games: "I was an athlete who stood up and said this policy is wrong, unnecessary, and harmful to athletes." In 2015, the IOC ditched the restrictions that prevented trans men from competing against men, opening a clear path for trans athletes. Mosier dubbed the rule change "a pivotal moment" not only for him—because it paved a path for him to compete for Team USA in the World Championship—but "for every transgender athlete." He said, "My greatest achievement is opening doors for other athletes to be themselves and to compete at a high level."

The backlash has been fierce, and the IOC caved to the pressure. In November 2021, it released a framework of guiding principles that sports federations were encouraged to use as they created their own policies for transgender athletes. In theory, these sports federations were not supposed to ban transgender athletes merely on the assumption that trans women enjoyed inherent advantages. The IOC stated that any federation's policy should be buttressed by serious, peer-reviewed, scientific evidence. In practice, however, international sports federations have passed an uneven patchwork of rules that all but ban trans athletes from participating and fail to apply academic research as a scientific foundation.

Then, in March 2026, the IOC banned transgender women athletes from competing in the Olympics. The new policy imposes mandatory genetic testing on all female athletes. As Mosier and Erika Lorshbaugh wrote in the *Los Angeles Times*, the effects of this policy extend far beyond trans athletes. "About 1 in 50 people are born with natural variations in their sex traits—also known as intersex (referred to in the IOC policy as having a 'difference of sex development')," they wrote. "These variations don't confer athletic advantages. But many young women will be disqualified because they have such variations—and many of them don't even know it."

Transgender people have been fighting for their rights for decades. Recall the famous Stonewall rebellion in 1969 in New York, the radical ACT UP protests around HIV and AIDS that began in the 1980s, and the fight for same-sex marriage in the 21st century. Chris Mosier's athlete activism continues this righteous tradition. Trans visibility is vital, and Mosier is putting himself under the media spotlight to advance the cause. "Sport is a vehicle for social change," he said. "Sport has that power to bring people together over a shared cause, a shared goal. The change that we create in sports can most certainly ripple out into the rest of the world."

BILQIS
ABDUL-QAADIR
FRENCH

BILQIS ABDUL-QAADIR

Bilqis Abdul-Qaadir confronted an excruciating choice between her passion for basketball and her devotion to Islam. Whichever path she picked, she faced a poignant pivot that would define her life.

Abdul-Qaadir's soul-searching came in response to a manufactured crisis, one she never should have been forced to contemplate. The either-or was foisted on her by FIBA, the world's governing body for basketball, which had a rule on its books stating that "players shall not wear equipment (objects) that may cause injury to other players." The hijab that Abdul-Qaadir wore while she smashed Massachusetts' all-time high school points record, averaged more than 14 points a game playing NCAA Division I basketball, and beat President Barack Obama in a game of one-on-one at the White House was deemed an injury risk by the powerbrokers who set the rules for international basketball. "Sometimes," she said, "you have no choice but to stand up for what you believe and who you are."

Abdul-Qaadir was born and raised in Springfield, Massachusetts, coincidentally the birthplace of basketball, where in 1891 physical education teacher James Naismith invented the game. She started playing basketball at age four and quickly set the goal to play professionally. Competition was engraved into daily life; she is one of eight siblings—four sisters and three brothers—and all played basketball. The basketball court became a space where Abdul-Qaadir could just be. "Everyone thinks it is just a sport," she said at the Toronto International Film Festival in 2019, "but when I play basketball, I think about nothing. It takes me out of real life."

In *Life Without Basketball*, the film that chronicles her battle with FIBA, Abdul-Qaadir said, "It's hard being a young Muslim woman in America. You have to be strong." She added, "It takes strength to walk outside and look different than everybody else." At times, she considered not covering just so she could play the game she loved, but she realized that larger forces were in play. Put simply, the fight was bigger than basketball. "In this world I think conforming is one of the worst things you can possibly do," she said.

After graduating from Indiana State University, Abdul-Qaadir aspired to play professionally in the WNBA. When that didn't pan out, she set her sights abroad. But because FIBA's ban on donning head coverings on the basketball court applied to most international professional leagues, Abdul-Qaadir's religious practice would make her ineligible to play. FIBA enforced this rule despite having found zero instances of injury caused by a hijab, yarmulke, or turban. In contrast, FIFA, soccer's international governing body, had officially ditched its own hijab ban in 2014. If FIFA's notorious president Sepp Blatter could see the light on the failed policy—he had once suggested that the popularity of women's soccer could grow if FIFA were to "Let the women play in more feminine clothes like they do in volleyball. They could, for example, have tighter shorts"—then certainly it wasn't too much to ask FIBA's executives to amend their evidence-free policy.

Rather than sit and sulk, Abdul-Qaadir chose to take a stand. As the Toronto-based sportswriter Shireen Ahmed—a fellow Muslim woman who wears a hijab—put it: "Policing of women's bodies is a norm in the sports world but the indomitable women have had enough and are fighting back." That's exactly what Abdul-Qaadir did.

But that didn't mean it was easy. Her identity was anchored in basketball. "I don't know who I am," she admitted during the initial stages of her exclusion from the game. "I can comfortably say that because I was so used to being a basketball player. I want to be great. I want to do something that can affect people still and I think that basketball always gave me that thing to affect people." Tearing up, she asked, "Am I anybody without basketball? Am I still myself?"

Abdul-Qaadir teamed up with Indira Kaljo, a Bosnian-American hoopster who played college basketball at Tulane University where she opted not to wear her hijab while on the court. Kaljo also played professionally in Saudi Arabia where FIBA's rules did not apply. They championed a Change.org petition demanding that FIBA reconsider its rules and, using the hashtag #FIBAAllowHijab, got more than 130,000 people to sign in support. More than thirty prominent athletes also signed a separate letter expressing solidarity, including Olympic fencer Ibtihaj Muhammad (featured in the following chapter), tennis star Billie Jean King, and numerous players from the WNBA and NBA. For Abdul-Qaadir, this support, as well as the moral support provided by President Obama, "was a huge boost for my confidence to keep pushing."

Activist gumption won the day. In May 2017, feeling the pressure, FIBA voted to amend its rules, making it legal to wear a hijab and other religious head coverings while playing basketball. The revamped rule went into effect in October 2017. By this time, Abdul-Qaadir had been sidelined for nearly four years. But in the meantime, she had been coaching, teaching, and serving as the athletic director at a private school in Tennessee while also starting a nonprofit organization called Muslim Girls Ball Too designed to empower girls and young women.

Once FIBA issued the decision to end the ban, Abdul-Qaadir experienced cross-cutting feelings. On one hand, she described the decision to end the ban as "long overdue," adding that it felt "surreal . . . to be a part of history, to be a part of change." On the other hand, the victory forced her to confront the issue afresh, rekindling feelings of grief that she had worked hard to overcome.

In a way, Bilqis Abdul-Qaadir was *not* forced to choose between her passion for basketball and her Islamic faith. For starters, she eventually played in an international tournament in Dubai, scoring 38 points in her first game back on the court. But more broadly, staying true to her religious beliefs and fueled by her love of the sport, she dismantled a barrier so other Muslim women and girls will not have to endure the discrimination she was forced to confront. "The experience gave me a new view on the meaning of sacrifice," she stated. "Sacrifice isn't always negative. I sacrificed for the bigger picture, and now I see the fruits of that sacrifice."

Abdul-Qaadir pushed for justice for future generations of girls to play basketball while wearing the hijab. Her courage in the face of institutional power and bureaucratic obstinacy scythed a path for all to excel, securing equal access and opportunity for players of diverse faiths and traditions. President Obama got it right when he said, "Bilqis is an inspiration not simply to Muslim girls, she's an inspiration to all of us."

IBTIHAJ
MUHAMMAD
FRENCH

IBTIHAJ MUHAMMAD

The barrier breakers of sport wield remarkable cultural power that can ripple out through society, etching hope into the social landscape. Fencer Ibtihaj Muhammad was the first US athlete to compete in the Olympic Games wearing a hijab and the first hijab-wearing medal winner. Muhammad won bronze in team fencing at the 2016 Olympics in Rio de Janeiro. Even before she participated in the 2016 Games, *Time* magazine had placed her on their list of "The 100 Most Influential People."

Major world leaders also took notice of Muhammad's accomplishments and influence. "There are some firsts that show the world America's greatness doesn't come only from high scores or fast times, but from our diversity and our tolerance and our open hearts," said President Barack Obama at a White House event honoring US Olympians after the Rio Games. "This summer's fencer, Ibtihaj Muhammad, became the first American female athlete to compete in the Olympic Games in a hijab. And that's important."

Nothing came easy for Muhammad. Her road to Rio was riddled with Islamophobia and racism. Born in Newark in 1985, she moved to the New Jersey suburb of Maplewood at a young age. During middle school she endured a steady stream of abuse, ranging from offensive questions about "wearing a tablecloth on her head" to physical attacks.

Meanwhile, Muhammad excelled at a variety of sports. Eventually she settled on fencing, in part because her mother realized that the modest uniform would cover her in ways that conformed to the principles of Islam. Twelve years old when she first lifted a fencing sword, Muhammad plunged herself into the sport and proved herself a quick learner. By 2005, at age nineteen, she was a Junior Olympics national champion.

The Rio Olympics took place during a hotly contested presidential campaign battle between Hillary Clinton and Donald Trump. Trump's public criticisms of Muslims fomented abuse and even hate, which were directed at Muhammad in equal measure as she prepared for the Games. During the Rio Olympics, Muhammad admitted that, at times, she did not feel safe as a Black Muslim woman living in the United States. This generated a vitriolic right-wing backlash, but, in truth, Muhammad experienced death threats both before and after the 2016 Rio Olympics.

And yet, Muhammad did not back down in the face of Islamophobia. "To not speak up and defend who I was as a Muslim American and what I stood for was not an option," she wrote. She even went on the offensive, stating that the Trump administration "does not believe in facts and obfuscates the truth . . . This administration has deemed athletes un-American for peacefully exercising their most fundamental freedoms. This administration has declared war on the media and decries the work of a free press as 'fake news.'"

Even inside the sports world, racism and Islamophobia often got in the way of some people appreciating Muhammad for who she is: a strong, proud, Black, Muslim woman. Higher-ups in the fencing world, and even the US Olympic community, were also unable to overcome their own discriminatory inclinations. Muhammad's coach on Team USA, as well as some teammates, snubbed her through clumsy microaggressions—"Do you use a magic carpet to pray?"—and petty efforts to exclude her from team meals. As her success on the fencing mat increased, the more she was ostracized. "The treatment I received from my coach and the rest of the team," Muhammad revealed in her memoir *Proud: My Fight for an Unlikely American Dream*, "grew increasingly harsh and cruel." As the heartless behavior intensified, it only steeled her resolve to continue competing.

As elite Muslim athletes, Ibtihaj Muhammad and basketball player Bilqis Abdul-Qaadir had an extra hurdle: maintaining their high-level performance during Ramadan when Muslims observe the practice of fasting from sunrise to sundown. Ramadan marks the ninth month on the Islamic calendar, the time when, according to the Islamic belief system, God delivered the Qur'an. Since the Muslim calendar year is slightly shorter than its Gregorian counterpart, Ramadan commences around 10 to 12 days earlier each year; this means that, over a 33-year cycle, it takes place during every season. For elite athletes, blending self-restraint with extreme exertion can be a real challenge, especially during the summer months when 18-hour days of light are not uncommon. After all, fasting entails abstaining from food and drink—even the water that athletes casually sip to replenish during competition.

To ward off dehydration, Muhammad's strategy was to guzzle water during the night hours, even at the expense of sleep. Unfortunately, neither the Olympic coaching staff nor her teammates made the effort to understand why she was fasting and what it meant to her spiritually: "The coach and my teammates had no sympathy for my situation," she wrote. When she labored from a lack of energy, her coach dubbed her "lazy"; she let it slide for fear of enacting the stereotype of the angry Black woman. "I was always conscious about how I would come across to my white teammates and my white coach in this mostly white sport," she noted. She even described the toxic training atmosphere as "psychological warfare."

Muhammad is not only aware of the racial factors that influence who becomes a fencer and who does not but also the class dynamics. "Fencing is such an expensive sport that you don't find it in the public school system and you don't find it in inner-city neighborhoods where there are large minority populations," she said. "Because of limited access to the sport it does become very one-note in terms of its participants. It is people who have money and predominantly people who come from white families."

And yet, Muhammad overcame it all and won bronze at the 2016 Rio Olympics. She explained, "Standing on an Olympic podium in Brazil, seeing my country's flag rise above me, I felt an overwhelming sense of triumph, defying society's limited expectations, breaking barriers placed in front of me because of the color of my skin and my faith. At the highest level of sport, I proudly represented, competed and medaled for my country."

In the wake of her success at the Rio Olympics, Mattel toy company honored Muhammad by creating a Barbie doll in her likeness. After years of criticism that Barbie dolls perpetuated white supremacy and unhealthy body ideals, the manufacturer shifted gears in the 1990s and began creating Barbies featuring a range of races and ethnicities. But the Barbie celebrating Muhammad was the first-ever to don a hijab. This was extremely meaningful to Muhammad and spotlights how athlete activists play a vital role in expanding cultural representation.

Ibtihaj Muhammad is a role model whose actions transcend her individual trials and tribulations. And for her, the final chapter has yet to be written. "Just as I defied the odds to make it to the Olympics in a sport that didn't have a place for me," she wrote, "I will continue to fight—to use all of my resources—for equality, justice, and peace."

COLIN
KAEPERNICK
FRENCH

COLIN KAEPERNICK

When an NFL quarterback takes a knee, it's usually to end a football game. But when San Francisco 49ers quarterback Colin Kaepernick knelt on September 1, 2016, during the national anthem of a preseason matchup in San Diego, he started a generational movement.

Born on November 3, 1987, in Milwaukee, Wisconsin, Kaepernick moved with his adoptive family to California when he was four. As a student at John H. Pitman High School in Turlock, California, he excelled in football, basketball, and baseball, all while maintaining a 4.0 grade point average.

After high school, Kaepernick's academic excellence and skills as a quarterback earned him a scholarship to the University of Nevada, Reno. There, as signal-caller for the Wolf Pack, he not only threw for 10,000 yards and rushed for another 4,000—a first in Division I history—but he also earned another 4.0 GPA, graduating with a degree in business management. Thanks to his record-breaking resume and exceptional talents, he was drafted by the San Francisco 49ers in 2011, where he quickly made his mark as a dynamic, electrifying player.

But becoming an NFL star did not diminish Kaepernick's moral conscientiousness or sense of social responsibility. His life story provided context for understanding his decision to kneel as continuing the work of America's nonviolent civil rights activists. As Kaepernick explained to reporters after that game, kneeling had nothing to do with disrespect to America, its flag, or its service members. Quite the opposite. Kneeling was a form of loyal criticism, meant to convey "that we have a lot of issues in this country that we need to deal with. We have a lot of people that are oppressed. We have a lot of people that aren't treated equally, aren't given equal opportunities. Police brutality is a huge thing that needs to be addressed. There are a lot of issues that need to be talked about, need to be brought to life, and we need to fix those."

The idea to kneel, furthermore, came from a former Green Beret, Nate Boyer. Boyer thought kneeling could evoke overtones of honor and solidarity, given that it is the stance soldiers take at a fallen brother or sister's grave or while resting alert on patrol. Based on a conversation with Boyer, Kaepernick adopted the symbol in hope of conveying the loyal criticism that fueled his protest of the country's chronic injustices. Soon, other athletes began joining Kaepernick's protest.

Backlash came swiftly too. Many jumped at the chance to criticize the 49ers quarterback. One of the most persistent, Republican presidential nominee Donald Trump, tweeted about Kaepernick no less than thirty-seven times, calling for owners to fire any player who kneeled. His remarks helped catalyze fan boycotts, burned jerseys, and threats, even as Kaepernick emphasized his protest was a call for justice, not disrespect. Such a vitriolic response was anything but surprising. In *The Heritage: Black Athletes, a Divided America, and the Politics of Patriotism*, journalist Howard Bryant draws a direct line from Kaepernick to earlier athletes like Mahmoud Abdul-Rauf, who was suspended by the NBA in 1996 for refusing to stand for the anthem, and Craig Hodges, a three-point champion iced out of the NBA after delivering a letter on racial injustice to President George H. W. Bush. Yet despite precedent and the obvious risks to his career, Kaepernick persisted. His protest movement grew.

In a telling example, little more than a year after Kaepernick first knelt, the entire Dallas Cowboys squad, otherwise known as "America's Team," knelt before their game against the Arizona Cardinals, team owner Jerry Jones among them. The impact extended far beyond the NFL, sparking a grassroots movement of conscience among young athletes across the country. In *The Kaepernick Effect*, Dave Zirin documents how high school and college players began kneeling, often in the face of strong opposition from their own communities.

In terms of immediate impact, Kaepernick's knee hitting the turf sent shockwaves of change and awareness throughout the NFL. His protest, however, also revealed deeply troublesome fault lines in the league's moral priorities. Consider: in February of 2013, Colin Kaepernick led the San Francisco 49ers to the Super Bowl. There, they fell just shy of defeating a Baltimore Ravens team that was powered by a dominant defense. Kaepernick had established himself as a leader, a game-changer, and a franchise quarterback. One respected veteran commentator even predicted that Kaepernick might well become an all-time great quarterback. The three years between then and the protests of 2016 had tempered expectations for Kaepernick's career, but even amidst volatile changes within the 49ers organization, he continued to show the skill, abilities, and commitment that made him elite.

And yet, after March 2017, when Kaepernick opted out of his contract with the 49ers (who would have released him otherwise), he could find no work in the NFL, despite his impressive resume and skill set. The league's doors were suddenly all closed. Kaepernick was used to exposing weaknesses in NFL defenses. Now, simply by being a free agent, he was exposing ethical weaknesses in the NFL itself. Was it possible that a player could be qualified in skill, character, resume, and competitive drive, and yet be denied opportunity because he had become a symbol of peaceful protest?

Kaepernick remained unsigned throughout 2017 under circumstances he and his legal team considered suspicious. In October, they filed a grievance accusing the NFL of colluding to keep him out of the league. The filing alleged that multiple head coaches and general managers expressed interest in signing him, only to suddenly withdraw without explanation. Teams that could have benefited from his skill set instead hired retired or long-inactive quarterbacks to lucrative contracts, often without granting Kaepernick a tryout or interview. The NFL strongly denied claims of collusion against the former 49ers player. However, the league later reached a financial settlement with Kaepernick in February of 2019 for an undisclosed amount.

Many assumed the settlement signaled the end of ongoing tensions between the league and the ostracized quarterback. Not so. Instead, the NFL organized a highly publicized but strangely orchestrated workout for Kaepernick—held on short notice, under restrictive conditions, and on a Saturday during the season, when key scouts would be absent. Kaepernick's camp viewed the offer with skepticism and hosted an independent session instead. The event, like much of the league's response, seemed more about managing optics than offering a real path back. In the end, Kaepernick decided to parlay the date and location proposed by the NFL into a showcase hosted by his staff, open to all media, with no need for special legal wranglings. Other than a flurry of speculations in the media about the strangeness of it all, nothing came of the day.

For football fans who hoped to see more of what Kaepernick's talent could accomplish, the injustice done to him is a loss for all. Then again, even in exile from the NFL, Kaepernick has given the sporting world—and the world at large—something far more valuable than the thrill of watching him play. He cast a spotlight on how far the United States has yet to go in becoming the just society dreamed of in our charter. And the way the NFL and many of its fans reacted to his protest exposed the nation's readiness to reject even the most respectful criticism of its moral failings. "Kaepernick's choice," David Steele observes, "is a turning point in American history. . . . One man's choice called a league, a sport, an athletic universe, and a universe in total to declare their choices as well, and to do it quickly."

But beyond the societal choices Kaepernick brought to light, he quietly showed the world a passion for decency and justice that transcends not only sports, but also the glory, fame, and wealth a league like the NFL can offer. And he has continued to build upon that example through a variety of endeavors: producing films and television projects, delivering keynote speeches, funding community initiatives, and leading the Know Your Rights Camp, which helps young people understand their legal protections, cultural history, and opportunities for education and activism. Through it all, he is challenging a new generation to pursue excellence in everything while seeking justice for everyone. As the 2019 Emmy-winning Nike ad put it, with words written across a portrait of Kaepernick's face: "Believe in something, even if it means sacrificing everything."

NAOMI
OSAKA
FRENCH

NAOMI OSAKA

It may seem that Naomi Osaka's voice came out of nowhere.

Osaka arrived on the professional tennis circuit as a soft-spoken sixteen-year-old in 2014. The multiethnic millennial was born in Japan to a Haitian-American father and a Japanese mother and was raised primarily in New York and Florida. After watching Venus and Serena Williams compete at the 1999 French Open, Osaka's father decided to start teaching his two daughters tennis. Mari, the oldest, was perhaps more comfortable with media and with being herself in the fairly homogenous tennis world, but it was her shy younger sister, Naomi, who would play her way into the spotlight.

Osaka worked her way up the Women's Tennis Association (WTA) circuit, competing under the Japanese flag and making a name for herself as a quiet competitor with a loud tennis game. In 2016 the teenage Osaka was named the WTA's Newcomer of the Year. Off the court, however, she was still finding her footing. Describing herself as "extremely shy," Osaka was known for her quirky media interviews where she was polite but seemingly perplexed that anyone wanted to hear from her at all. Yet, over the next five years, she would grow to be one of the most outspoken athletes in tennis and beyond.

Naomi Osaka's journey as an athlete activist began when she asserted her identity in ways that challenged simplistic racial logics in both the United States and Japan. Later, Osaka became increasingly vocal against anti-Black and anti-Asian racism and engaged in multiple meaningful protests. She has also emerged as a mental-health advocate.

As Osaka's visibility increased, so too did the scrutiny over her racial, ethnic, and national identity. Osaka won her first major title at Indian Wells in 2018. A few months later she won her first Grand Slam tournament—the US Open—defeating her idol, Serena Williams. Osaka's tears during the trophy presentation jumpstarted important debates about gender, emotions, and sportsmanship. This moment, and the media storm that followed, reignited conversations around Osaka's identity.

Osaka was used to the perplexed stares, probing questions, and "shocked look on people's faces" when she arrived at tennis tournaments. Was she Black? Japanese? American? Haitian? Why does she speak English so well? Does she understand Japanese? The questions persisted, with many attempting to slot Osaka in a manageable box. The tennis star met this curiosity with a clear and unbothered version of the same answer: "I don't really think that I'm three separate, like, mixes of whatever. I just think that I'm me."

Following the 2018 US Open, which was dominated by media accounts of Serena Williams's dispute with an umpire, an Australian illustrator published a racist image depicting the end of the match. In the image, Williams was drawn as a toddler having a tantrum using stereotypical exaggerated Black minstrel features. Osaka was drawn as her foil: an innocent, petite, lighter-skinned woman with blonde hair. This "whitewashing" of Osaka would be the first of many images that distanced her from her Blackness or that downplayed parts of her identity.

Osaka's refusal to let the media mute any facet of her identity was particularly significant in Japan, where her ascendency was widely celebrated. Motoko Rich argued in *The New York Times* that Osaka's win "help[ed] to challenge Japan's longstanding sense of racial purity and cultural identity." Many *hafu,* or mixed-race Japanese people, saw the embrace of Osaka as an opportunity to spark a larger dialogue about inclusion in Japanese society. As one agent noted, Osaka was already positioned to move "beyond sports" as an "ambassador of change" because of the symbolic space she occupied. Yet in 2020, Osaka would merge the symbolic with direct action to become one of the boldest activist athletes of the time.

In 2020, the COVID-19 pandemic brought the world to a halt, including tennis. A social epidemic—the heightened visibility of state-sanctioned violence against Black people in the United States—stoked an explosive summer of protest, grassroots activism, and political change. During this pause, Osaka said that she was "able to take more personal time, more time for self-reflection, more time to understand and witness the world around [her]." The result? An increasingly vocal Naomi Osaka who was extra-motivated to speak out.

In the days after George Floyd was killed by police, Osaka flew to Minneapolis to protest, mourn, and support activists who were taking to the streets. Shortly thereafter, she published an article explaining why she went and what she stands for: "In the past few months, I've re-evaluated what's actually important in my life. It's a reset that perhaps I greatly needed. I asked myself, 'If I couldn't play tennis, what could I be doing to make a difference?' I decided it was time to speak up."

Osaka began regularly using social media to speak out about systemic racism and police brutality. She particularly saw herself as someone well-positioned to help the message go global, connecting conversations about anti-Blackness in the United States and Japan. "From Oslo to Osaka, from Tallahassee to Tokyo, protests have included people of all races and ethnicities," Osaka wrote. "There were even Black Lives Matter marches in Japan—something many of us would never have expected or imagined possible."

When Jacob Blake was shot multiple times by police in Kenosha, Wisconsin, later that summer, Osaka watched the Milwaukee Bucks refuse to play a game. As the wildcat strike spread across the NBA and the WNBA, athletes from other sports began to follow suit. Before her semifinal match at the Western and Southern Open in Flushing Meadows, New York, Osaka posted a statement in English and Japanese to her social media pages. "Before I am a[n] athlete, I am a black woman. And as a black woman I feel as though there are much more important matters at hand that need immediate attention, rather than watching me play tennis." Osaka was refusing to play.

Osaka's dissent sent shockwaves through the tennis world. The protest actions taken in sports that were racially diverse were becoming increasingly common. However, Osaka's action in a predominantly white sport was a significant development in the growing visibility of athlete activism. In response to her refusal to play, the tournament paused for two days. When Osaka returned to the court, she was more committed than ever to speak out. She was not going to "shut up and play."

When she showed up for the US Open a few weeks later, she carried that commitment with her—literally. Osaka arrived at the tournament with seven masks, one for each round, all bearing the name of a Black person who had been killed by police or vigilantes: *Breonna Taylor, Elijah McClain, Ahmaud Arbery, Trayvon Martin, George Floyd, Philando Castile, Tamir Rice.* "I didn't feel that with all that I was seeing in the world around me I could just show up and play as if nothing had happened, as if lives were not unjustly taken," she explained. Osaka wore every single mask en route to her second US Open Championship. The win solidified Naomi Osaka as the future of tennis and as a prominent athlete activist.

Because the origin site of COVID-19 appeared to be Wuhan, China, the pandemic led to a rise in anti-Asian racism. Osaka once again used her position to speak out. She remained steadfast in her vocal support of protests and equally committed to raising awareness and advocating for change. Her voice would continue to evolve as well. Within tennis she advocated for increased access to the sport, challenged the homogeneity of those who covered and governed the sport, and called out gender disparities in the game.

Then, in the spring of 2021, Osaka publicly discussed her struggle with anxiety and depression. To protect her mental health, she revealed that she would not be taking part in the mandatory post-match press conferences, accepting whatever fine was given to her. The backlash from organizers of the French Open was quickly supported by all four Grand Slam tournaments, which united to threaten Osaka and to compel her participation. Yet, in the face of this pressure, Osaka returned to her strategy of refusal, pulling out of the French Open entirely. For her, there were more important things than playing tennis.

Osaka demonstrated a willingness to prioritize her mental health, her politics, and her full humanity over trophies and accolades. Olympian swimmer Michael Phelps, who has been outspoken about mental health, applauded Osaka. "It doesn't matter if you're number one in the world or the average Joe, anybody can go through this," Phelps said, calling her actions "a game-changer in mental health moving forward."

JORDAN
MARIE DANIEL
FRENCH

JORDAN MARIE BRINGS THREE WHITE HORSES WHETSTONE (NÉE DANIEL)

"Running for me has been about culture, legacy, history, and continuing this tradition of our family," explains Jordan Marie Brings Three White Horses Whetstone (née Daniel). Her mother, Terra Betha Brings Three White Horses Daniel, was a sprinter, but Whetstone inherited her love of distance running from her grandfather,

Nyal Brings, a hall-of-fame runner at the University of South Dakota. Whetstone is Kul Wicasa Lakota and grew up a citizen of the Kul Wicasa Oyate Nation in South Dakota, where her grandfather introduced her to running. When their family moved to Maine when Jordan was nine, running became an important outlet. Maine was so different from the life on the reservation that Whetstone had known. For the first time she felt *different.* As she experienced racism and isolation, running offered a respite. Whetstone found community in her cross-country team. But it would be a few years until she realized that running could also be a form of advocacy.

Growing up as an Indigenous person in Maine, Whetstone experienced what she describes as a "cultural identity crisis." She began to feel her Indigeneity differently. She had a front-row seat to racism and inequality, both interpersonal and structural. "It's two different worlds," Whetstone explained to *Sports Illustrated.* "You have to learn how to still stay connected to back home, and you have to learn how to fit in in this modern, colonized world."

Remaining close with her grandfather helped her stay connected to her identity. While she once was embarrassed about her long Lakota name, she came to embrace it. Jordan's grandfather had maintained his Native culture despite being sent to the boarding schools that endeavored to "civilize" Native youth. Between 1869 and the 1960s, the federal government forcibly removed Native children from their homes and sent them to boarding schools run by the government or churches. In these schools, Native children were forbidden to speak their languages, forced to cut their hair, and made to change their clothes. It was cultural genocide designed as education. Yet her grandfather had held on to his name, and now Jordan would use it as an anchor.

She continued to run competitively through college, and at the University of Maine she majored in political science and minored in Native Studies. She was determined to go to Washington, DC, and work on the issues impacting Native communities. Upon graduation she did just that. Whetstone was still running competitively, but her working world and running world seemed like disconnected parts of her life.

In 2016, however, Whetstone was invited to run the Boston Marathon to raise funds and awareness for an organization called Running Strong for American Indian Youth. Running Strong was founded by Billy Mills, an Oglala Lakota man who won gold in the 10,000-meter competition at the 1964 Olympics in Tokyo. Mills was also a friend and old training partner of Jordan's grandfather. While Whetstone was preparing to run the marathon, she began to think of other ways she could use running to bring awareness to issues facing tribal communities.

Later that year Whetstone was approached by a friend who thought she would be the ideal person to help organize a running event in DC to bring attention to ongoing protests against the Dakota Access Pipeline (DAPL). The construction of the DAPL had been fiercely opposed by the Standing Rock Sioux since the proposed placement of the pipeline encroached on sacred tribal sites and threatened the safety of their water supply. By 2016, the issue had gone national with the Standing Rock Sioux and their allies staging a number of protests to raise awareness and disrupt the construction. Nick Estes, a historian and citizen of the Lower Brule Sioux Tribe, noted that "DAPL's trespass through unceded treaty territory and the militarized crackdown on Water Protectors was made to look like self-defense—settlers in the fort, surrounded by hostile natives." But activists like Whetstone had other ideas. Jordan helped organize a Water for Life rally that welcomed Standing Rock youth who were running from Standing Rock to Washington, DC. She rallied supporters to greet the runners and join them in carrying a petition directly to the US Army Corps of Engineers and the Supreme Court.

From that point on, Whetstone saw the opportunity to connect running and advocacy. In 2017 she founded Rising Hearts, an organization advocating for and facilitating connection between Indigenous groups. So, in 2019, when Wings of America, a Boston nonprofit supporting Native runners and youth, asked if she would partner with them and run the marathon, Rising Hearts embraced the opportunity.

When Whetstone runs marathons, she highlights Missing and Murdered Indigenous Women (MMIW), or what some call Missing and Murdered Indigenous People (MMIP) or Missing and Murdered Indigenous Relatives (MMIR). Across the United States and Canada, there is an epidemic of violence impacting Native women and girls and Indigenous people more generally. Native women are disproportionately more likely to experience violence at alarming rates, and while the statistics are staggering. The fact that the numbers are also woefully underreported only exacerbates the problem. Efforts to raise awareness about MMIW, MMIP, and MMIR have increased over the years, and Whetstone's subtle protests have highlighted the issue.

Leading up to the 2019 marathon, however, Whetstone felt like her protest needed to be bigger than numbers on her bib. So she wrote *MMIW* in big letters all over her body, and on her face she painted a big red handprint—a symbol for MMIW—that covered her mouth. For each of the 26 miles of the marathon, Whetstone recited a name of a missing Native woman and offered up a prayer. For the last 0.2 miles she said a prayer to her grandfather. "It felt really good to end that race for him," she said afterward. "I hope I'm making him proud, not only by crossing the finish line but also by the way I'm carrying Indian Country with me."

Whetstone's protest went viral. It helped to amplify the conversation around MMIW and offered a blueprint for others who wanted to use running spaces as a platform for change. After seeing Whetstone's protest, Rosalie Fish, a high school runner and a member of the Cowlitz Tribe, replicated it during the Washington state track and field championships later that year. Whetstone said her ongoing goal is "to keep spreading this message and to keep raising awareness, to bring allies, to get everyone to support those that have been doing this work for decades, to support the families who have loved ones missing or murdered, and to continue this ongoing conversation and to paint the message clear that there are dangers and targets for Indigenous women and Black women, especially, and folks of color."

Rising Hearts features specific running-based advocacy programs that use running as a platform for change, but it also seeks to transform the running community itself. The Running on Native Lands initiative, for instance, partners with race directors and running clubs to use land acknowledgments and other tools to connect runners to the land, history, and community. Additionally, Whetstone has turned to filmmaking to create works that explore and promote Native voices, athletic activism, environmental work, and diverse perspectives. In 2024, Vice President Kamala Harris recognized Whetstone for her efforts.

Jordan Marie Brings Three White Horses Whetstone's life work chimes with scholar Wesley C. Hogan's insight that "Young people have ignited original approaches" to activism and advocacy, "picking up on the age-old rhythms" of different "cultures and political traditions and splicing them together anew, evidence yet again of the powerful strands of what we can call our remix culture." When reflecting on her past activism and ongoing commitment to advocacy, Whetstone told *Sports Illustrated*, "I want to assert our presence and to show we're still here. A lot of people have never met a Native American and think they belong only in textbooks. This is an opportunity for myself and other Indigenous runners who are sponsored athletes and are just in this world and outdoor running environment to say, 'Hey, we're still here.' Enough is enough." Whetstone added, "We've been sitting on the backburners for too long, feel like we've been forgotten and are invisible, but we're not taking it anymore. We're putting ourselves out there, helping support other indigenous peoples and bringing them to a platform where their voices can be heard."

SOURCES

INTRODUCTION

Bass, Amy. *Not the Triumph but the Struggle: The 1968 Olympics and the Making of the Black Athlete*. Minneapolis: University of Minnesota Press, 2002.

Brown, Letisha Engracia Cardoso, A. Lamont Williams, Amanda N. Schweinbenz, and Ann Pegoraro. "A Perfect Storm: Black Feminism and Women's National Basketball Association Black Athlete Activism." *Sociology of Sport Journal* 42, no. 1 (March 2025): 1–9.

Cooper, Joseph N. *A Legacy of African American Resistance and Activism Through Sport*. New York: Peter Lang, 2021.

Davis, Amira Rose. "No More Games: Understanding the Latest Wave of Athletic Activism." *The American Historian*, September 2020. https://www.oah.org/tah/issues/2020/history-for-black-lives/no-more-games-understanding-the-latest-wave-of-athletic-activism/.

Davis, Ben. *9.5 Theses on Art and Class*. Chicago: Haymarket Books, 2013.

Edwards, Harry. *The Revolt of the Black Athlete*. Urbana: University of Illinois Press (1969) 2017.

"LeBron James: Racist Graffiti Incident Shows 'I Still Have a Lot of Work to Do.'" ESPN, February 15, 2018. https://www.espn.com/nba/story/_/id/22458566/cleveland-cavaliers-lebron-james-golden-state-warriors-kevin-durant-talk-president-donald-trump-racial-divide-country/.

Moore, Louis. *We Will Win the Day: The Civil Rights Movement, the Black Athlete, and the Quest for Equality*. Santa Barbara, CA: Praeger, 2017.

Obama, Barack. "Remarks by the President Welcoming the 2016 USA Olympic and Paralympic Teams." The White House, September 29, 2016. https://obamawhitehouse.archives.gov/the-press-office/2016/09/29/remarks-president-welcoming-2016-usa-olympic-and-paralympic-teams/.

O'Neill, Francis, Geoff Dickson, Tim Ströbel, and Ashleigh-Jane Thompson. "Elite Athlete Activism, Advocacy, and Protest: A Scoping Review." *European Sport Management Quarterly* 25, no. 1 (2025): 145–73.

Romero, Iliana Limón. "Angel City FC Wears Shirts Declaring Itself 'Immigrant City Football Club.'" *Los Angeles Times*, June 14, 2025. https://www.latimes.com/sports/soccer/angel-city-fc/story/2025-06-14/angel-city-fc-wears-shirts-declaring-itself-immigrant-city-football-club/.

Sullivan, Emily. "Laura Ingraham Told LeBron James to Shut Up and Dribble; He Went to the Hoop." NPR, February 19, 2018. https://www.npr.org/sections/thetwo-way/2018/02/19/587097707/laura-ingraham-told-lebron-james-to-shutup-and-dribble-he-went-to-the-hoop/.

"World Athletics Publishes Online Abuse Study Covering Tokyo Olympic Games." World Athletics, November 25, 2021. https://worldathletics.org/news/press-releases/online-abuse-study-athletes-tokyo-olympic-games.

JIM THORPE

"America First as Olympics End." *New York Times*, July 16, 1912, 1.

Andrejev, Alex. "Katie Ledecky, Jim Thorpe Named Presidential Medal of Freedom Recipients." *The Athletic*, May 3, 2024.

Bergvall, Erik, and Swedish Olympic Committee. *The Official Report of the Olympic Games of Stockholm 1912*. Stockholm: Wahlström and Widstrand, 1913.

Boykoff, Jules. *Power Games: A Political History of the Olympics*. London: Verso, 2016.

Brundage, Avery. Collection. International Centre for Olympic Studies. Western University. London, Ontario, Canada.

Buford, Kate. *Native American Son: The Life and Sporting Legend of Jim Thorpe*. New York: Alfred A. Knopf, 2010.

Eskenazi, Gerald. "Jim Thorpe's Olympic Medals Are Restored." *New York Times*, October 14, 1982, A1.

Floyd, Jacob. "On Hollywood Boulevard: Native Community in Classical Hollywood." *Journal of Cinema and Media Studies* 60, no. 2 (Winter 2021): 163–68.

"Indian Thorpe in Olympiad." *New York Times*, April 28, 1912, C9.

Jenkins, Sally. "Why Are Jim Thorpe's Olympic Records Still Not Recognized?" *Smithsonian Magazine*, July 2012. https://www.smithsonianmag.com/history/why-are-jim-thorpes-olympic-records-still-not-recognized-130986336/#W1HqwDHhoXgixxpf.99/.

Lindsey, Robert. "Thorpe's Medals Returned." *New York Times*, January 19, 1983, B13.

Maraniss, David. "At Long Last, the Olympic Injustice Done to Jim Thorpe Is Corrected." *Washington Post*, July 17, 2022. https://www.washingtonpost.com/opinions/2022/07/17/olympics-finally-fix-jim-thorpe-wrong/.

Maraniss, David. *Path Lit by Lightning: The Life of Jim Thorpe*. New York: Simon and Schuster, 2022.

McCallum, Jack. "The Regilding of a Legend." *Sports Illustrated*, October 25, 1982.

Silvershein, Andrew. "What You May Not Know About the Legendary Jim Thorpe." *Bleacher Report*, June 22, 2021. https://bleacherreport.com/articles/1075531-what-you-may-not-know-about-the-legendary-jim-thorpe/.

JACKIE ROBINSON

"Breaking Barriers: Jackie Robinson's Baseball Journey." *Jackie Robinson*. Accessed January 18, 2026. https://jackierobinson.com/about/baseball/.

Dorinson, Joseph, and Joram Warmund. *Jackie Robinson: Race, Sports, and the American Dream*. London: Routledge, 1998.

Dreier, Peter. "The Real Story of Baseball's Integration That You Won't See in *42*." *The Atlantic*, April 11, 2013. https://www.theatlantic.com/entertainment/archive/2013/04/the-real-story-of-baseballs-integration-that-you-wont-see-in-i-42-i/274886/.

Long, Michael G. *First Class Citizenship: The Civil Rights Letters of Jackie Robinson*. New York: Holt Paperbacks, 2008.

"MLB Rosters Feature 251 International Players." MLB, March 29, 2019. https://www.mlb.com/news/mlb-rosters-feature-251-international-players/.

Ott, Tim. "The Activism of Jackie Robinson." *Biography*, September 11, 2020. https://www.biography.com/news/jackie-robinson-civil-rights-facts/.

Rampersad, Arnold. *Jackie Robinson: A Biography*. New York: Alfred A. Knopf, 1997.

Robinson, Jackie, and Alfred Duckett. *I Never Had It Made: An Autobiography of Jackie Robinson*. New York: Ecco, 2003.

Robinson, Jackie, and Spike Lee. *Baseball Has Done It*. New York: Ig Publishing, 2005.

Tygiel, Jules. *The Jackie Robinson Reader: Perspectives on an American Hero*. New York: Plume, 1997.

ALTHEA GIBSON

Brown, Ashley. "How Althea Gibson Faced Racial Barriers—Even as a Tennis Champion." *History,* June 26, 2025. https://www.history.com/news/althea-gibson-tennis-racial-barrier/.

Brown, Ashley. *Serving Herself: The Life and Times of Althea Gibson.* New York: Oxford University Press, 2023.

Gibson, Althea. *I Always Wanted to Be Somebody.* New York: Harper and Row, 1958.

Gibson, Althea, and Richard Curtis. *So Much to Live For.* New York: Putnam, 1968.

Lansbury, Jennifer H. *A Spectacular Leap: Black Women Athletes in Twentieth-Century America.* Fayetteville: University of Arkansas Press, 2014.

EARLENE BROWN

"Bias Mars Girls AAU Meet." *Chicago Defender*, July 11, 1960.

Davis, Michael, D. *Black American Women in Olympic Track and Field: A Complete Illustrated Reference.* Jefferson, NC: McFarland and Co., 1992.

"Earlene Brown, 220 Pounds of Joy, Makes Friends for U.S. in Moscow." *The Washington Post and Times Herald*, July 27, 1958.

Gissendanner, Cindy Himes. "African American Women Olympians: The Impact of Race, Gender, and Class Ideologies, 1932–1968." *Research Quarterly for Exercise and Sport* 67, no. 2 (1996): 172–82.

"The Inside Track: Russ Laughs at Earlene." *Los Angeles Mirror*, September 3, 1960, 7.

"'I Was Scared Silly' Says Earlene Brown." *Los Angeles Times*. November 23, 1956.

Jacobs, Karen Folger. "Earlene Brown: Down from Olympia." *Essence*, May 1979.

"Our American Way?" *Los Angeles Sentinel*, July 14, 1960.

WILMA RUDOLPH

Davis, Michael, D. *Black American Women in Olympic Track and Field: A Complete Illustrated Reference.* Jefferson, NC: McFarland and Co., 1992.

"Double Sprint Champion Didn't Walk Until She Was 8." *Philadelphia Inquirer*, September 10, 1960.

Grizzard, Lauren. "The Fastest Woman in the World: Wilma Rudolph." Tennessee State Museum. February 25, 2021. https://tnmuseum.org/junior-curators/posts/the-fastest-woman-in-the-world-wilma-rudolph/.

Lansbury, Jennifer H. *A Spectacular Leap: Black Women Athletes in Twentieth-Century America.* Fayetteville: University of Arkansas Press, 2014.

Parrish, Tim. "'Wilma' Movie Showing this Weekend in Clarksville." *Leaf Chronicle*. February 13, 2015. https://www.theleafchronicle.com/story/news/local/clarksville/2015/02/13/wilma-movie-showing-weekend-clarksville/23383119/.

Rudolph, Wilma. *Wilma*. New York: Signet, 1977.

"Wilma: I Have Enjoyed My Stay." *Daily Graphic*, May 2, 1963, 11.

"Wilma Denies 'Broke' Stories." *Chicago Daily Defender*, March 29, 1969, 29.

"Wilma Proves They're Not All 'Muscle Molls.'" *Philadelphia Inquirer*, September 10, 1960.

Wilson, Wayne. "Wilma Rudolph: The Making of an Icon." In *Out of the Shadows: A Biographical History of African American Athletes*, edited by David K. Wiggins. Fayetteville: University of Arkansas Press, 2006, 207–21.

PAUL ROBESON

Bryant, Howard. *The Heritage: Black Athletes, a Divided America, and the Politics of Patriotism*. Boston: Beacon Press, 2018.

"Dr. Bunche and Mr. Robeson." *New York Times*, July 19, 1949, 28.

Duberman, Martin. *Paul Robeson*. New York: The New Press, 1989.

Dyson, Michael Eric. *Making Malcolm: The Myth and Meaning of Malcolm X*. New York: Oxford University Press, 1995.

Gordon, A. J. "U.S. Cancels Robeson's Passport After He Refuses to Surrender It." *New York Times*, August 4, 1950, 1.

Horne, Gerald. *Paul Robeson: The Artist as Revolutionary*. London: Pluto Press, 2016.

Kirshenbaum, Jerry. "Paul Robeson: Remaking a Fallen Hero." *Sports Illustrated*, March 27, 1972.

Lewis, Anthony. "Supreme Court, 5–4, Voids Passport Denials to Reds." *New York Times*, June 17, 1958, 1.

Neruda, Pablo. "Ode to Paul Robeson." In *Paul Robeson: The Great Forerunner*, edited by *Freedomways*. New York: Dodd, Mead and Co., (1965) 1978, 244–50.

Robeson, Paul. *Here I Stand*. Boston: Beacon Press, (1958) 1971.

Smith, Ronald A. "The Paul Robeson-Jackie Robinson Saga and a Political Collision." *Journal of Sport History* 6, no. 2 (Summer 1979): 5–27.

Wiggins, David K., and Patrick B. Miller, eds. *The Unlevel Playing Field: A Documentary History of the African American Experience in Sport*. Urbana: University of Illinois Press, 2003.

EROSEANNA "ROSE" ROBINSON

"The Anger That Inflamed Route 40." *Life Magazine*, December 8, 1961, 32–39.

Davis, Amira Rose. "Sixty Years Ago She Refused to Stand for the Anthem." *ZORA* (blog), September 26, 2019. https://zora.medium.com/sixty-years-ago-she-refused-to-stand-for-the-anthem-cf443b4e75c7/.

"Girl Track Star Refuses to go to Russia." *Jet Magazine*, July 31, 1958, 54.

Lukas, J. Anthony. "Trouble on Route 40." *The Reporter*, October 26, 1961, 41–44.

Morten, Baker E. "Ex-Track Star Continues Jail Fast; Pickets Protest." *Daily Defender*, February 3, 1960.

Rider, Toby C., and Kevin B. Witherspoon, eds. *Defending the American Way of Life: Sport, Culture, and the Cold War.* Fayetteville: University of Arkansas Press, 2018.

Robinson, Eroseanna. "Three Months at Alderson Prison." *The Catholic Worker* 27, no. 3 (October 1960).

Wiggins, David, ed. *Out of the Shadows: A Biographical History of African American Athletes.* Fayetteville: University of Arkansas Press, 2006.

Wolcott, Victoria W. *Race, Riots, and Roller Coasters: The Struggle over Segregated Recreation in America.* Reprint ed. Philadelphia: University of Pennsylvania Press, 2014.

MUHAMMAD ALI

Ali, Muhammad, with Hana Yasmeen Ali. *The Soul of a Butterfly: Reflections on Life's Journey.* New York: Simon and Schuster, 2004.

Anderson, Mae. "Muhammad Ali Wasn't Always 'The Greatest' at Sponsorships." Associated Press, June 8, 2016. https://apnews.com/general-news-36bf17fb23dc43a8be625c49a04d1237/.

Becker, Bill. "Cassius Clay Knocks Out Moore in 4th Round After Flooring Him 3 Times." *New York Times*, November 16, 1962, 52.

Bryant, Howard. *The Heritage: Black Athletes, a Divided America, and the Politics of Patriotism.* Boston: Beacon Press, 2018.

Cooper, Joseph N. *Black Sporting Resistance: Diaspora, Transnationalism, and Internationalism.* New Brunswick, NJ: Rutgers University Press, 2025.

Dankowski, Terra. "Jonathan Eig Pulls No Punches." *American Libraries*, June 24, 2018. https://americanlibrariesmagazine.org/blogs/the-scoop/jonathan-eig-pulls-no-punches/.

"The Draft: Ali Up." *Time*, February 25, 1966. https://time.com/archive/6628963/the-draft-ali-up/.

Early, Gerald. "Introduction: Tales of the Wonderboy." In *The Muhammad Ali Reader*, edited by Gerald Early. New York: Rob Weisbach Books, 1998, vii–xx.

Eskenazi, Gerald. "Champion Shows Baffling Traits." *New York Times*, May 26, 1965, 54.

Eskenazi, Gerald. "World Boxing Group Threatens to Lift Clay's Heavyweight Title." *New York Times*, March 23, 1964, 37.

Garcia, Ahiza. "Muhammad Ali: A Brand Known Around the World." CNN, June 4, 2016. https://www.cnn.com/2016/06/04/news/muhammad-ali-brand-under-armour/.

Garrow, David J. *Bearing the Cross: Martin Luther King, Jr., and the Southern Christian Leadership Conference.* New York: Harper Perennial, 1986.

Kane, Martin. "Ready to Go in Rome." *Sports Illustrated*, August 29, 1960, 10–12. https://archive.org/details/Sports-Illustrated-1960-08-29/page/n21/mode/2up/.

Kang, Stephanie. "Adidas Gets Artsy with Its US Ads." *Wall Street Journal*, February 5, 2004. https://www.wsj.com/articles/SB107593404088320951/.

Lipsyte, Robert. "Boxing Chief Backs Curbs." *New York Times*, April 1, 1964, 36.

Marqusee, Mike. *Redemption Song: Muhammad Ali and the Spirit of the Sixties.* 2nd ed. London: Verso, 2005.

"Muhammad Ali: The Dream," *Time*, March 22, 1963. https://time.com/3537815/muhammad-ali-dead-the-dream/.

"Muhammad Ali Memorial: Chief Sidney Hill and Chief Oren Lyons." WLKY (Louisville), June 10, 2016. https://www.wlky.com/article/muhammad-ali-memorial-chief-sidney-hill-and-chief-oren-lyons/3600192#/.

"1996 Atlanta Opening Ceremonies—Lighting of the Cauldron." Posted September 12, 2006, by julius923, YouTube, 8 min., 15 sec. http://www.youtube.com/watch?v=5TaITzi64Sw.

Patterson, Floyd, and Milton Gross. "I Want to Destroy Clay." *Sports Illustrated*, October 19, 1964, 42–61. https://archive.org/details/Sports-Illustrated-1964-10-19/page/n45/mode/2up/.

Remnick, David. *King of the World: Muhammad Ali and the Rise of an American Hero.* New York: Random House, 1998.

"Scorecard (The Black Muslim Hope)." *Sports Illustrated*, March 16, 1964, 8. https://archive.org/details/Sports-Illustrated-1964-03-16/page/n15/mode/2up.

Tuckner, Howard M. "'Man, It's Great to Be Great.'" *New York Times*, December 9, 1962, 134.

United States v. Clay. 386 F. Supp. 926. U.S. District Court for the Southern District of Texas, July 14, 1969. https://law.justia.com/cases/federal/district-courts/FSupp/386/926/2307863/.

Zirin, Dave. *What's My Name, Fool? Sports and Resistance in the United States.* Chicago: Haymarket Books, 2005.

BILLIE JEAN KING

"Billie Jean King." International Tennis Hall of Fame. Accessed June 2025. https://www.tennisfame.com/hall-of-famers/inductees/billie-jean-king/.

Brake, Deborah L. *Getting in the Game: Title IX and the Women's Sports Revolution.* New York: New York University Press, 2010.

Brandman, Mariana. "Billie Jean King." National Women's History Museum, June 2021. https://www.womenshistory.org/education-resources/biographies/billie-jean-king/.

Deford, Frank. "Mrs. Billie Jean King!" *Sports Illustrated*, May 19, 1975. https://vault.si.com/vault/1975/05/19/mrs-billie-jean-king/.

"Equality." BillieJeanKing.com. Accessed June 2025. https://www.billiejeanking.com/equality/.

King, Billie Jean, with Kim Chapin. *Billie Jean*. New York: Harper and Row, 1974.

King, Billie Jean, Johnette Howard, and Maryanne Vollers. *All In: An Autobiography.* New York: Knopf, 2021.

Thompson, Caitlin. "Billie Jean King: The First Female Athlete-Activist." *New York Times*, August 17, 2021. https://www.nytimes.com/2021/08/17/books/review/all-in-billie-jean-king.html/.

Ware, Susan. *Game, Set, Match: Billie Jean King and the Revolution in Women's Sports.* Chapel Hill: The University of North Carolina Press, 2015.

TOMMIE SMITH

Brundage, Avery. Collection. International Centre for Olympic Studies. Western University. London, Ontario

Daley, Arthur. "The Incident." *New York Times*, October 20, 1968, S2.

Musburger, Brent. "Bizarre Protest by Smith, Carlos Tarnishes Medals." *Chicago American*, October 17, 1968, 43.

Obama, Barack. "Remarks by the President Welcoming the 2016 USA Olympic and Paralympic Teams." The White House, September 29, 2016. https://obamawhite

house.archives.gov/the-press-office/2016/09/29/remarks-president-welcoming-2016-usa-olympic-and-paralympic-teams/.
Smith, Tommie, with David Steele. *Silent Gesture: The Autobiography of Tommie Smith*. Philadelphia: Temple University Press, 2007.
Smith, Tommie, Derrick Barnes, and Dawud Anyabwile. *Victory. Stand! Raising My Fist for Justice*. New York: Norton Young Readers, 2022.
Stevens, Tess. "Olympians, Activists Tommie Smith, John Carlos Show Support of Former SF 49er Colin Kaepernick." ABC News, November 15, 2017. https://abc7news.com/sports/olympians-activists-tommie-smith-john-carlos-show-support-for-kaepernick/2653950/.
Whyno, Stephen. "Colin Kaepernick Gets Support from Tommie Smith, John Carlos." Associated Press, September 29, 2016. https://www.thestar.com/sports/2016/09/29/colin-kaepernick-gets-support-from-tommie-smith-john-carlos.html/.
Zaccardi, Nick. "Tommie Smith, John Carlos Part of US Olympic Hall of Fame Class." NBC Sports, September 23, 2019. https://www.nbcsports.com/olympics/news/tommie-smith-john-carlos-us-olympic-hall-of-fame/.

JOHN CARLOS

Boykoff, Jules. "Olympian John Carlos Reflects on His Controversial Stand for Human Rights." *Street Roots*, December 6, 2012. https://news.streetroots.org/2012/12/06/olympian-john-carlos-reflects-his-controversial-stand-human-rights/.
Brundage, Avery. Collection. International Centre for Olympic Studies. Western University. London, Ontario, Canada.
Carlos, John, with Dave Zirin. *The John Carlos Story: The Sports Moment that Changed the World*. Chicago: Haymarket Books, 2011.
Carrington, Ben. *Race, Sport, and Politics: The Sporting Black Diaspora*. London: Sage, 2010.
Daley, Arthur. "The Incident." *New York Times*, October 20, 1968, S2.
Edwards, Harry. *The Revolt of the Black Athlete*. Urbana: University of Illinois Press, (1969) 2017.
Hartmann, Douglas. *Race, Culture, and the Revolt of the Black Athlete: The 1968 Olympic Protests and Their Aftermath*. Chicago: University of Chicago Press, 2003.
Jacoby, Joie, and Maura Brandt, dirs. *Return to Mexico City*. New York: MaggieVision; Bristol, CT: ESPN Films, 2009.
"65 Athletes Support Boycott of Olympics on S. Africa Issue." *New York Times*, April 12, 1968, 28.

WYOMIA TYUS

"Black Women's Athletic Activism." Posted October 22, 2020, by Penn State College of the Liberal Arts. YouTube, 1 hour, 30 min., 11 sec. https://www.youtube.com/watch?v=aQAVjhdDSmU.

Burtka, Allison Torres. "Wyomia Tyus: The Original Athlete Activist Hiding in Plain Sight." *The Guardian*, December 23, 2021. https://www.theguardian.com/sport/2021/dec/23/wyomia-tyus-athlete-activism-usa-olympics/.

Carlson, Lewis H., and John J. Fogarty. *Tales of Gold: An Oral History of the Summer Olympic Games Told by America's Gold Medal Winners*. Chicago: Contemporary Books, 1987.

"Episode 53: Happy Birthday to BIAD, with Special Guests Wyomia Tyus and Elena Delle Donne." *Burn It All Down*, May 8, 2018. https://www.burnitalldownpod.com/episodes/53.

Lanker, Brian, and Maya Angelou. *I Dream a World.* New York: Harry N. Abrams, 1999.

Lansbury, Jennifer H. *A Spectacular Leap: Black Women Athletes in Twentieth-Century America.* Fayetteville: University of Arkansas Press, 2014.

Longman, Jeré. "A Quiet Demonstration and a Long Shadow." *New York Times*, June 17, 2021. https://www.nytimes.com/2021/06/17/sports/olympics/wyomia-tyus-athlete-protests-racism.html.

"Olympic Politics." *Los Angeles Times,* October 22, 1968.

Organizing Committee of the Games of the XIX Olympiad. *Official Report of the 1968 Olympic Games*. Vol. 3, *The Games*. Los Angeles: LA84 Foundation, 1969.

Swidwa, Kathy. "Athletes to Discuss History, Future of Black Women's Protest in Sports." Pennsylvania State University, April 15, 2021.

Terzakis, Elizabeth, and Wyomia Tyus. *Tigerbelle: The Wyomia Tyus Story.* Illus. ed. Brooklyn, NY: Akashic Books, 2018.

MAHMOUD ABDUL-RAUF

Abdul-Rauf, Mahmoud, with Nick Chiles. *In the Blink of an Eye: An Autobiography*. New York: Kaepernick Publishing, 2022.

Agyemang, Kwame J. A., John N. Singer, and Anthony J. Weems. "'Agitate! Agitate! Agitate!': Sport as a Site for Political Activism and Social Change," *Organization* 27, no. 6 (June 2010), 952–68. https://doi.org/10.1177/1350508420928519.

Bass, Amy. *Not the Triumph but the Struggle: The 1968 Olympics and the Making of the Black Athlete*. Minneapolis: University of Minnesota Press, 2002.

"Former NBA Player Mahmoud Abdul-Rauf on New Autobiography and Athlete Activism (Full Stream 10/17)." Posted October 17, 2022, by Washington Post Live. YouTube, 31 min., 30 sec. https://www.youtube.com/watch?v=lTvJlo3tst8.

Grewal, Zareena. "Lights, Camera, Suspension." In *Black Routes to Islam*, edited by Manning Marable and Hisham Aidi. New York: Palgrave Macmillan, 2009, 191–205.

Litvin, Yoav. "Mahmoud Abdul-Rauf's Diagnosis of America," *CounterPunch*, October 21, 2022. https://www.counterpunch.org/2022/10/21/mahmoud-abdul-raufs-diagnosis-of-america/.

"Mahmoud Abdul-Rauf | Ep 169." Posted February 9, 2023, by All the Smoke (Showtime Basketball). YouTube, 1 hour, 29 min., 38 sec. https://www.youtube.com/watch?v=IRconmok61Y.

Singer, Mike. "'Unfinished Business': Why Nuggets Great Mahmoud Abdul-Rauf Left Teammates, Coaches Wanting More." *Denver Post*, May 17, 2020. https://www.denverpost.com/2020/05/17/mahmoud-abdul-rauf-nuggets-career-anthem-protest/.

Smith, Earl, Angela J. Hattery, Marissa Kiss, and Katelyn E. Foltz. "Re-Conceptualizing Kaepernick's Kneeling Protests and His Banishment From the NFL as an Infringement on His 'Right to Work.'" *Journal of Black Studies* 54, no. 6 (September 2023): 469–489

Wolff, Alexander. "Can't Hold This Tiger: Chris Jackson of LSU Is Having the Best Season of Any First-Year Guard in History." *Sports Illustrated*, February 20, 1989. https://vault.si.com/vault/1989/02/20/cant-hold-this-tiger-chris-jackson-of-lsu-is-having-the-best-season-of-any-first-year-guard-in-history/.

Zirin, Dave. *A People's History of Sports in the United States: 250 Years of Politics, Protest, People, and Play*. New York: The New Press, 2008.

GWEN BERRY

Berry, Gwen. "This Should Make You Uncomfortable." *The Players' Tribune*, October 21, 2021. https://www.theplayerstribune.com/posts/gwen-berry-olympics-usa-track-and-field-racial-injustice/.

"Black Women Athletes Speak Out." *Burn It All Down*, June 5, 2020. https://www.burnitalldownpod.com/episodes/black-women-athletes-speak-out/.

Davis, Amira Rose. "Black Women on Team USA Have to Play Two Games." *Slate*, July 24, 2021. https://slate.com/culture/2021/07/olympics-black-women-athletes-gwen-berry-shacarri-richardson-swim-caps.html/.

Demby, Gene. "The Butterfly Effects of Ferguson." NPR, August 11, 2016. https://www.npr.org/sections/codeswitch/2016/08/11/489494015/the-butterfly-effects-of-ferguson/.

"Freedom Schools." SNCC Digital Gateway. Accessed July 5, 2025. https://snccdigital.org/inside-sncc/culture-education/freedom-schools/.

Kilgore, Adam. "After Shaping Protest Rules in the US, Gwen Berry Has a New Sponsor and an Eye on Tokyo." *Washington Post*, June 23, 2021. https://www.washingtonpost.com/sports/olympics/2021/06/21/gwen-berry-puma-us-olympic-track-trials/.

Scoby, Ashley. "With Fist Raised, Olympic Track and Field Star Gwen Berry Determined to Make a Difference." ESPN, September 26, 2019. https://www.espn.com/espnw/life-style/story/_/id/27699003/with-fist-raised-olympic-track-field-star-gwen-berry-determined-make-difference/.

BILL RUSSELL

"Bill Russell." *Biography*, August 11, 2022. https://www.biography.com/athletes/bill-russell/.

"Bill Russell." StatMuse. Accessed July 8, 2025. https://www.statmuse.com/nba/player/bill-russell-3211/.

"Bill Russell Seasons." StatMuse. Accessed July 8, 2025. https://www.statmuse.com/nba/ask/what-are-bill-russell-finals-stats-by-year/.

Bodanza, Mark C. *Ten Times a Champion: The Story of Basketball Legend Sam Jones.* Bloomington, IN: iUniverse, 2016.

Eig, Jonathan. *Ali: A Life*. New York: Simon & Schuster, 2017.

Eig, Jonathan. "The Cleveland Summit and Muhammad Ali: The True Story." Andscape, June 1, 2017. https://andscape.com/features/the-cleveland-summit-muhammad-ali/.

Goudsouzian, Aram. *King of the Court: Bill Russell and the Basketball Revolution.* Berkeley: University of California Press, 2010.

Makin, Ken. "Commentary: The Day the Sports World's Bubbles Burst." *Christian Science Monitor*, August 3, 2022. https://www.csmonitor.com/USA/Society/2020/0828/Commentary-The-day-the-sports-world-s-bubbles-burst/.

Merlino, Doug. "Bill Russell, Civil Rights Hero and Inventor of Airborne Basketball." *Bleacher Report*, April 29, 2011. https://bleacherreport.com/articles/682589-bill-russell-civil-rights-hero-and-inventor-of-airborne-basketball/.

Powell, Michael. "When Black Athletes Stood Up for Muhammad Ali." *New York Times*, June 4, 2017. https://www.nytimes.com/2017/06/04/sports/muhammad-ali-black-athletes.html.

Russell, Bill, and Alan Steinberg. *Red and Me: My Coach, My Lifelong Friend*. New York: Harper, 2009.

Whalen, Thomas J. *Dynasty's End: Bill Russell and the 1968–69 World Champion Boston Celtics*. Boston: Northeastern University Press, 2005.

KAREEM ABDUL-JABBAR

Abdul-Jabbar, Kareem. "The Importance of Athlete Activists." *Time*, November 18, 2015. https://time.com/4114002/kareem-abdul-jabbar-athlete-activists/.

Abdul-Jabbar, Kareem, and Raymond Obstfeld. *Becoming Kareem: Growing Up On and Off the Court*. New York: Little, Brown Books for Young Readers, 2017.

Abdul-Jabbar, Kareem, and Raymond Obstfeld. *We All Want to Change the World: My Journey Through Social Justice Movements from the 1960s to Today*. New York: Crown, 2025.

Anderson, Devery S., and Julian Bond. *Emmett Till: The Murder That Shocked the World and Propelled the Civil Rights Movement*. Jackson: University Press of Mississippi, 2017.

Eig, Jonathan. "The Cleveland Summit and Muhammad Ali: The True Story." Andscape, June 1, 2017. https://andscape.com/features/the-cleveland-summit-muhammad-ali/.

El Tecolote Staff. "Athleticism and Activism: Kareem's Dual Legacies on Display." *El Tecolote*, September 8, 2016. http://eltecolote.org/content/en/sports-2/athleticism-and-activism-kareems-dual-legacies-on-display/.

"Emmett Till's Death Inspired a Movement." The Smithsonian National Museum of African American History and Culture. Accessed June 2025. https://nmaahc.si.edu/blog-post/emmett-tills-death-inspired-movement/.

"Exclusive Kareem Abdul-Jabbar Rare Legacy Auction." Kar33m, February 13, 2019. https://kareemabduljabbar.com/auction/.

"Lessons from a Legend: Abdul-Jabbar on a Life of Activism." *News from Brown* (Brown University), October 16, 2017. https://www.brown.edu/news/2017-10-16/abdul-jabbar/.

ARTHUR ASHE

"About Arthur Ashe." Arthur Ashe Student Health and Wellness Center (UCLA). Accessed July 2025. https://www.studenthealth.ucla.edu/about/arthur-ashe-biography.

Arsenault, Raymond. *Arthur Ashe: A Life.* New York: Simon and Schuster, 2018.

"Arthur Ashe." International Tennis Hall of Fame. Accessed June 2025. https://www.tennisfame.com/hall-of-famers/inductees/arthur-ashe/.

Ashe, Arthur, and Arnold Rampersad. *Days of Grace: A Memoir.* New York: Ballantine Books, 1994.

Crawford, E. J. "Black History Month Legends: Arthur Ashe." USTA, February 13, 2017. https://www.usta.com/en/home/stay-current/national/black-history-month-legends—arthur-ashe.html.

Duster, Chandelis. "Robert E. Lee Statue on Historic Virginia Street Removed." CNN, September 8, 2021. https://www.cnn.com/2021/09/08/politics/robert-e-lee-statue-richmond-virginia-removal/index.html.

Hall, Eric Allen. *Arthur Ashe: Tennis and Justice in the Civil Rights Era.* Baltimore: Johns Hopkins University Press, 2014.

Markel, Howard. "Arthur Ashe's Other Great Serve? As Activist for Health." *PBS News Hour*, July 10, 2021. https://www.pbs.org/newshour/health/arthur-ashes-other-great-serve-as-activist-for-health/.

Miller, Rex, and Sam Pollard, dirs. *Citizen Ashe.* New York: Magnolia Pictures, 2021. Amazon Prime.

NOTAH BEGAY III

Begay, Notah, III. Interview by Jules Boykoff, May 22, 2023.

Brady, Erik. "Notah Begay: Snyder's Redskins Foundation a 'Gimmick.'" *USA Today*, April 22, 2014. https://www.usatoday.com/story/sports/nfl/redskins/2014/04/22/daniel-snyder-team-name-controversy-foundation-notah-begay/8014797/.

Churchill, Ward. *Kill the Indian, Save the Man: The Genocidal Impact of American Indian Residential Schools.* San Francisco: City Lights Books, 2004.

Davis-Delano, Laurel R., Renee V. Galliher, and Joseph P. Gone. "Native Appropriation in Sport: Cultivating Bias Toward Native American Indians." *Race and Social Problems* 15, no. 4 (December 2023): 395–407.

Davis-Delano, Laurel R., Joseph P. Gone, and Stephanie A. Fryberg. "The Psychosocial Effects of Native American Mascots: A Comprehensive Review of Empirical Research Findings." *Race Ethnicity and Education* 23, no. 5 (September 2020): 613–33.

Deloria Jr., Vine. *Custer Died for Your Sins: An Indian Manifesto*. Norman: University of Oklahoma Press, (1969) 1988.

"Diabetes and American Indians/Alaska Natives." Office of Minority Health, US Department of Health and Human Services. Accessed February 13, 2025. https://minorityhealth.hhs.gov/omh/browse.aspx?lvl=4&lvlid=33.

Farrey, Tom. "Notah Begay's Long Walk." ESPN, June 3, 1999. http://www.espn.com/otl/americans/begayprint.html.

Gray, Will. "Notah Begay: Navajo Community 'Decimated' by COVID-19 Crisis." Golf Channel, April 9, 2020. https://www.golfchannel.com/news/notah-begay-iii-navajo-community-decimated-covid-19-crisis/.

Kelliher, Allison. "Native Americans Have Experienced a Dramatic Decline in Life Expectancy During the COVID-19 Pandemic—But the Drop Has Been in the Making for Generations." *The Conversation*, February 3, 2023. https://theconversation.com/native-americans-have-experienced-a-dramatic-decline-in-life-expectancy-during-the-covid-19-pandemic-but-the-drop-has-been-in-the-making-for-generations-186729/.

King, C. Richard, ed. *Native Americans in Sports*. London: Routledge, (2004) 2015.

Steinberg, Dan. "Notah Begay Calls Redskins Nickname 'Institutionalized Degradation.'" *Washington Post*, February 25, 2013. https://www.washingtonpost.com/news/dc-sports-bog/wp/2013/02/25/notah-begay-calls-redskins-nickname-institutionalized-degradation/.

Virgen, Steve. "Begay Expresses Relief, Joy for Washington Retiring Nickname." *Albuquerque Journal*, July 13, 2020. https://www.abqjournal.com/1475569/begay-expresses-relief-joy-for-washington-retiring-nickname.html.

Woodward, Denni Dianne. "The Removal of the Indian Mascot of Stanford." Stanford Native American Cultural Center. Accessed July 2025. https://nacc.stanford.edu/about-nacc/history-timelines/stanford-mascot-timeline/removal-indian-mascot-stanford.

SERENA WILLIAMS

di Costanzo, Diane. "Milestones in Equality: Women Fight for—and Win—Changes to Ranking Rules for Pregnancy." US Open, June 28, 2023. https://www.usopen.org/en_US/news/articles/2023-06-28/milestones_in_equality_women_fight_forand_winchanges_ranking_rules_for_pregnancy.html.

Dorisca, Samantha. "Serena Williams Has Invested in 14 Companies that Have Reached Unicorn Status." AfroTech, April 4, 2024. https://afrotech.com/serena-williams-helped-14-companies-reach-unicorn-status/.

Eccleshare, Charlie. "Venus Williams Won the Fight for Equal Prize Money—That Is Her Greatest Wimbledon Legacy." *The Athletic*, July 3, 2023. https://theathletic.com/4663957/2023/07/03/venus-williams-wimbledon-equal-prize-money/.

Jones, Maya A. "Venus and Serena Williams Return Home to Compton to Give Back." Andscape, November 7, 2016. https://andscape.com/features/venus-and-serena-williams-return-home-to-compton-to-give-back/.

Li, David K. "Serena Williams Set to Be an Owner of New WNBA Team the Toronto Tempo." NBC, March 3, 2025. https://www.nbcnews.com/sports/wnba/serena-williams-set-owner-new-wnba-team-toronto-tempo-rcna194569/.

Martin, Lori Latrice. "Double Fault: Serena Williams and Tennis at the Intersection of Race and Gender." *The Western Journal of Black Studies* 42, nos. 3–4 (Fall-Winter 2018): 88–96.

"Nike Releases Full Ad Featuring Colin Kaepernick." Posted September 7, 2018, by Guardian Sport. YouTube, 1 min., 1 sec. https://www.youtube.com/watch?v=-grjIUWKoBA.

Nittle, Nadra. "The Serena Williams Catsuit Ban Shows That Tennis Can't Get Past Its Elitist Roots." *Vox*, August 28, 2018. https://www.vox.com/2018/8/28/17791518/serena-williams-catsuit-ban-french-open-tennis-racist-sexist-country-club-sport/.

Schultz, Jaime. "Reading the Catsuit: Serena Williams and the Production of Blackness at the 2002 U.S. Open." *Journal of Sports and Social Issues* 29, no. 3 (August 2005): 338–57.

"Sitting Down with the Legendary Serena Williams." CNN, April 16, 2024. https://www.cnn.com/videos/sports/2024/04/16/exp-serena-tennis-olympics-davies-041607asegi-cnni-sports-fast.cnn.

Spencer, Nancy E. "Sister Act VI: Venus and Serena Williams at Indian Wells: 'Sincere Fictions' and White Racism." *Journal of Sport and Social Issues* 28, no. 2 (May 2004): 115–35.

Williams, Richard, with Bart Davis. *Black and White: The Way I See It.* New York: Atria Books, 2017.

Williams, Serena. "I'm Going Back to Indian Wells." *Time*, February 4, 2015. https://time.com/3694659/serena-williams-indian-wells/.

Williams, Serena. "What My Life-Threatening Experience Taught Me About Giving Birth." CNN, February 20, 2018. https://www.cnn.com/2018/02/20/opinions/protect-mother-pregnancy-williams-opinion/index.html.

Williams, Serena, and Rob Haskell. "Serena Williams Says Farewell to Tennis on Her Own Terms—And in Her Own Words." *Vogue*, August 9, 2022. https://www.vogue.com/article/serena-williams-retirement-in-her-own-words/.

LEBRON JAMES

Beacham, Greg. "LeBron and Bronny James Make History as the NBA's First Father-Son Duo to Play Together." NBA, July 6, 2024. https://www.nba.com/news/lebron-bronny-james-make-history-play-together/.

Bembry, Jerry. "LeBron James Is the Most Powerful Voice in His Profession." Andscape, February 18, 2018. https://andscape.com/features/lebron-james-to-take-floor-for-nba-all-star-game-as-the-most-powerful-voice-in-his-profession/.

Cohen, Ben. "LeBron James Says Tweet Supporting Hong Kong Protests Was 'Misinformed.'" *Wall Street Journal*, October 14, 2019. https://www.wsj.com/articles/lebron-james-says-tweet-supporting-hong-kong-protests-was-misinformed-11571107697/.

Guthrie, Marisa. "LeBron James: 10 Projects on His Growing Hollywood Slate." *The Hollywood Reporter*, September 20, 2018. https://www.hollywoodreporter.com/lists/lebron-james-10-projects-his-growing-hollywood-slate-1145543/item/lebron-projects-shop-1145527/.

Jones, Ryan. *King James: Believe the Hype—The LeBron James Story.* New York: St. Martin's Griffin, 2005.

"LeBron James: 'Akron Ohio, We Did It Again!'" Sportsnet, October 11, 2020. https://www.sportsnet.ca/basketball/lebron-james-akron-ohio/.

Nadkarni, Rohan. "Is LeBron James Still Chasing Michael Jordan's Ghost?" *Sports Illustrated*, January 1, 2019. https://www.si.com/nba/2019/01/01/lebron-james-michael-jordan-warriors-lakers-greatest-player-all-time-debate/.

Saslow, Eli. "Lost Stories of LeBron, Part 1." ESPN, October 17, 2013. https://www.espn.com/nba/story/_/id/9825052/how-lebron-james-life-changed-fourth-grade-espn-magazine/.

Singer, Michael. "LeBron James: Opening School Is My Most Important Professional Accomplishment." *USA Today*, November 30, 2017. https://www.usatoday.com/story/sports/nba/2017/11/30/lebron-james-opening-school-most-important-professional-accomplishment/909374001/.

Windhorst, Brian. *LeBron, Inc.: The Making of a Billion-Dollar Athlete.* New York: Grand Central Publishing, 2019.

Zirin, Dave. "LeBron James's Politics Stop at the Water's Edge." *The Nation*, October 15, 2019. https://www.thenation.com/article/archive/lebron-james-china/.

MEGAN RAPINOE

Associated Press. "Megan Rapinoe Says She Will Respect US Soccer Policy for National Anthem." *The Guardian*, March 6, 2017. https://www.theguardian.com/football/2017/mar/06/megan-rapinoe-us-soccer-national-anthem-policy.

Bushnell, Henry. "Megan Rapinoe Is a 'Walking Protest.'" Yahoo! Sports, May 13, 2019. https://sports.yahoo.com/megan-rapinoe-is-a-walking-protest-162416461.html.

Carlisle, Jeff. "Megan Rapinoe: Off-Field Achievements Bigger than USWNT Titles." ESPN, September 23, 2023. https://www.espn.com/soccer/story/_/id/38472120/megan-rapinoe-field-achievements-bigger-uswnt-titles/.

Garcia, Michelle. "Megan Rapinoe: I'm Not Going to the Fucking White House." *Out*, June 26, 2019. https://www.out.com/sports/2019/6/26/megan-rapinoe-im-not-going-fucking-white-house.

Halloran, John. "Megan Rapinoe Kneels for Anthem at NWSL Match." *American Soccer Now*, September 4, 2016. http://americansoccernow.com/articles/megan-rapinoe-kneels-for-anthem-at-nwsl-match/.

Longman, Jeré. "For Megan Rapinoe, Boldness in the Spotlight Is Nothing New." *New York Times*, June 27, 2019. https://www.nytimes.com/2019/06/27/sports/megan-rapinoe-trump-world-cup.html.

"Megan Rapinoe Reaction | The Best FIFA Women's Player 2019." Posted September 23, 2019, by FIFA. YouTube, 5 min., 59 sec. https://www.youtube.com/watch?v=tMoTp_w41gw.

Murray, Caitlin. "'It's Just the Start': How World Cup Victory Affects USA's Fight for Equal Pay." *The Guardian*, July 9, 2019. https://www.theguardian.com/football/2019/jul/09/us-womens-soccer-team-equal-pay-us-soccer-world-cup/.

Murray, Caitlin. "Will the US Women's Soccer Team Win Their Battle for Equal Pay?" *The Guardian*, March 9, 2019. https://www.theguardian.com/football/2019/mar/09/will-the-us-womens-soccer-team-win-their-battle-for-equal-pay/.

Oxenham, Gwendolyn. "Why Megan Rapinoe's Brother Brian Is Her Greatest Heartbreak, and Hope." ESPN, July 7, 2019. https://www.espn.co.uk/football/fifa-womens-world-cup/story/3878587/why-megan-rapinoes-brother-brian-is-her-greatest-heartbreakand-hope/.

Peterson, Anne M., and Ronald Blum. "US Soccer Equalizes Pay in Milestone with Women, Men." Associated Press, May 18, 2022. https://apnews.com/article/us-soccer-equal-pay-65070aeodfb82598b2815295039dfd2d/.

Poe, Julia. "USWNT Star Megan Rapinoe Delivers Powerful Speech at 2019 FIFA Best Awards." *Orlando Sentinel*, September 23, 2019. https://www.orlandosentinel.com/2019/09/23/uswnt-star-megan-rapinoe-delivers-powerful-speech-at-2019-fifa-best-awards/.

Portwood, Jerry. "Fever Pitch." *Out*, July 2, 2012. https://www.out.com/travel-nightlife/london/2012/07/02/fever-pitch/.

Press Association. "Megan Rapinoe Refuses to Back Down over Donald Trump and White House." *The Guardian*, June 27, 2019. https://www.theguardian.com/football/2019/jun/27/megan-rapinoe-donald-trump-white-house/.

Rapinoe, Megan, with Emma Brockes. *One Life*. New York: Penguin Press, 2020.

Trump, Donald J. (@realDonaldTrump). "Women's soccer player, @mPinoe." Twitter, June 26, 2019, 10:42 a.m. https://twitter.com/realdonaldtrump/status/1143892326286266368/.

Wrack, Suzanne. "'You Can't Win Without Gay Players,' Says USA's World Cup Hero Megan Rapinoe." *The Guardian*, June 28, 2019. https://www.theguardian.com/football/2019/jun/28/cant-win-without-gays-usa-megan-rapinoe/.

MAYA MOORE

Berkman, Seth. "In a Pioneering Moment for the W.N.B.A., Players Unite in Protests Over Injustices." *New York Times*, October 15, 2016. https://www.nytimes.com/2016/10/16/sports/basketball/wnba-players-protests.html.

Cash, Meredith. "It's Time to Give the Women of the WNBA Their Flowers for the Roles They Play in Politics and Social Justice." *Business Insider*, January 18, 2021. https://www.businessinsider.com/wnba-players-deserve-recognition-on-off-court-warnock-loeffler-georgia-2021-1/.

Cox, Courtney M. *Double Crossover: Gender, Media, and Politics in Global Basketball.* Urbana: University of Illinois Press, 2025.

Gregory, Sean. "Maya Moore Was One of the WNBA's Biggest Stars. Then She Stepped Away to Fight for Justice." *Time*, March 5, 2020. https://time.com/5793243/maya-moore-basketball-justice/.

Hurd, Sean. "Maya Moore, the Game-Changer: 'This Is the Epitome of Using Your Platform.'" Andscape, July 2, 2020. https://andscape.com/features/maya-moore-game-changer-jonathan-irons-epitome-of-using-your-platform/.

Martin, Sloane. "A Year Without Maya: On the Lynx Star's Decision and How the Team Will Adjust." *New York Times*, February 11, 2019. https://www.nytimes.com/athletic/812283/2019/02/11/maya-moore-sitting-out-season-lynx-cheryl-reeve/.

Mathewson, Eryn, and Leah Asmelash. "Fighting for Social Justice Is in the WNBA's DNA." CNN, August 29, 2020. https://www.cnn.com/2020/08/29/us/wnba-social-justice-spt-trnd/.

Moore, Maya. "(In)Visibility." *The Players' Tribune*, May 1, 2015. https://www.theplayerstribune.com/articles/maya-moore-wnba-visibility/.

Moore, Maya. "The Shift." *The Players' Tribune*, February 6, 2019. https://www.theplayerstribune.com/articles/maya-moore-wnba-announcement/.

Shoichet, Catherine E., and Martin Jill. "Off-Duty Cops Walk Out over WNBA Players' Black Lives Matter Shirts." CNN, July 12, 2016. https://www.cnn.com/2016/07/12/us/wnba-minnesota-lynx-black-lives-matter-shirts/.

Streeter, Kurt. "Jonathan Irons, Helped by W.N.B.A. Star Maya Moore, Freed from Prison." *New York Times*, July 1, 2020. https://www.nytimes.com/2020/07/01/sports/basketball/maya-moore-jonathan-irons-freed.html.

Streeter, Kurt. "Maya Moore Left Basketball. A Prisoner Needed Her Help." *New York Times*, June 30, 2019. https://www.nytimes.com/2019/06/30/sports/maya-moore-wnba-quit.html.

Weese, Lukas. "The Beginning of a Dynasty: An Oral History of the Minnesota Lynx's 2011 WNBA Title." *Just Women's Sports*, June 21, 2021. https://justwomenssports.com/reads/the-beginning-of-a-dynasty-an-oral-history-of-the-minnesota-lynxs-2011-wnba-title/.

Wright, Mark W. "Maya Moore's Nike 'Wings' Poster Inspires 4-Year-Old Girl to See Female Athletes in a New Light." Andscape, June 6, 2018. https://andscape.com/features/maya-moores-nike-wings-poster-inspires-4-year-old-girl-to-see-female-athletes-in-a-new-light/.

CHRIS MOSIER

Barnes, Katie. *Fair Play: How Sports Shape the Gender Debates.* New York: St. Martin's Press, 2023.

Birrell, Susan, and Cheryl L. Cole. "Double Fault: Renee Richards and the Construction and Naturalization of Difference." *Sociology of Sport Journal* 7, no. 1 (1990): 1–21.

Deschamps, David, and Bennett Singer. *LGBTQ Stats: Lesbian, Gay, Bisexual, Transgender, and Queer People by the Numbers.* New York: The New Press, 2017.

Dreier, Frederick. "For Transgender Athlete, a Top Finish in New York Is Secondary," *New York Times*, August 5, 2011. https://www.nytimes.com/2011/08/06/sports/for-transgender-triathlete-a-top-finish-is-secondary.html.

Kurtzleben, Danielle. "House Passes the Equality Act: Here's What It Would Do." NPR, February 24, 2021. https://www.npr.org/2021/02/24/969591569/house-to-vote-on-equality-act-heres-what-the-law-would-do/.

Mosier, Chris. Interview by Jules Boykoff, March 12, 2021.

Mosier, Chris, and Erika Lorshbaugh. "A Sex Test for Olympic Contenders Harms All Women." *Los Angeles Times*, April 27, 2026. https://www.latimes.com/opinion/story/2026-04-27/olympics-women-genetic-testing.

Pruitt-Young, Sharon. "Canadian Soccer Player Quinn Becomes the First Out Trans and Nonbinary Gold Medalist." NPR, August 6, 2021. https://www.npr.org/2021/08/06/1025442511/canadian-soccer-player-quinn-becomes-first-trans-and-nonbinary-olympic-gold-meda/.

Trump, Donald J. Executive Order 14201. "Keeping Men Out of Women's Sports." The White House, February 5, 2025. https://www.whitehouse.gov/presidential-actions/2025/02/keeping-men-out-of-womens-sports/.

Webb, Karleigh. "Lia Thomas Wins NCAA Championship in 500 Freestyle." *Out Sports*, March 17, 2022. https://www.outsports.com/2022/3/17/22983857/lia-thomas-wins-ncaa-championship-in-500-freestyle/.

Zirin, Dave. *Edge of Sports*, podcast. "Chris Mosier: In Defense of Trans Athletes." SoundCloud, January 17, 2021. https://soundcloud.com/edgeofsports/chris-mosier-in-defense-of-trans-athletes/.

Zirin, Dave, and Jules Boykoff. "Why There Are No Trans Women Competing at the Paris Games." *The Nation*, July 25, 2024. https://www.thenation.com/article/society/trans-athletes-paris-olympics/.

BILQIS ABDUL-QAADIR

Abdul-Qaadir, Bilqis. Interview by Jules Boykoff, June 11, 2020.

Ahmed, Shireen. "After a Long Fight, FIBA Finally Lifts Its Ban on Religious Headwear." *Vice*, May 4, 2017. https://sports.vice.com/en_us/article/nz8bvg/after-a-long-fight-fiba-finally-lifts-its-ban-on-religious-headwear/.

Ahmed, Shireen. "Bilqis Abdul-Qaadir Is Fighting to Lift FIBA's Hijab Ban." *Teen Vogue*, March 27, 2017. https://www.teenvogue.com/story/bilqis-abdul-qaadir-fighting-fiba-hijab-ban/.

"Athlete Ally and Shirzanan Publish Open Letter Demanding FIBA Overturn its Hijab Ban." Athlete Ally, January 25, 2017. https://www.athleteally.org/athlete-ally-shirzanan-publish-open-letter-demanding-fiba-overturn-hijab-ban/.

Burton, Austin L. "FIBA Explains Article 4.4.2 Prohibiting Hijab." *Ummah Sports*, May 19, 2014. https://ummahsports.net/2014/05/19/fiba-explains-article-4-4-2-prohibiting-hijab/.

"End Ban on Head-Covering in International Basketball." Change.org. Accessed July 2025. https://www.change.org/m/end-ban-on-head-covering-in-basketball#about-movement/.

"*Life Without Basketball* with Bilqis Abdul-Qaadir." Posted November 18, 2019, by Toronto International Film Festival (TIFF). YouTube, 41 min., 59 sec. https://www.youtube.com/watch?v=LabXS7DHU1w.

O'Donnell, Tim, and Jon Mercer, dirs. *Life Without Basketball*. Gravitas Films, 2019.

"Women Footballers Blast Blatter." BBC, January 16, 2004. http://news.bbc.co.uk/sport2/hi/football/3402519.stm.

IBTIHAJ MUHAMMAD

Ahmed, Shireen. "Here's How 15 Hardcore Athletes Train During Ramadan." *BuzzFeed*, June 18, 2017. https://www.buzzfeednews.com/article/shireenahmed/athletes-fasting-during-ramadan/.

Chin, Elizabeth. "Ethnically Correct Dolls: Toying with the Race Industry." *American Anthropologist* 101, no. 2 (June 1999): 305–21.

Deb, Sopan. "Ibtihaj Muhammad: The Olympic Fencer Is Charting Her Own Path." *New York Times*, July 24, 2018. https://www.nytimes.com/2018/07/24/books/ibtihaj-muhammad-fencing-hijab-olympics.html.

Ellison, Keith. "Ibtihaj Muhammad." *Time*, April 21, 2016. https://time.com/collection-post/4301357/ibtihaj-muhammad-2016-time-100/.

Hall, Matthew. "Ibtihaj Muhammad: 'Being Made to Feel Different Is What Makes It All the More Difficult.'" *The Guardian*, July 27, 2018. https://www.theguardian.com/sport/2018/jul/27/ibtihaj-muhammad-fencing-hijab-olympics/.

Hines, Nico. "Ibtihaj Muhammad, Hijab-Wearing Olympic Star: I'm Not Safe in the US." *Daily Beast*, August 4, 2016. https://www.thedailybeast.com/ibtihaj-muhammad-hijab-wearing-olympic-star-im-not-safe-in-the-us/.

Muhammad, Ibtihaj. "Olympian: This Is What It Means to Be an American." CNN, July 23, 2018. https://www.cnn.com/2018/07/23/opinions/what-being-american-means-ibtihaj-muhammad-olympics-opinion/index.html.

Muhammad, Ibtihaj, with Lori L. Tharps. *Proud: My Fight for an Unlikely American Dream*. New York: Hachette Books, 2018.

Obama, Barack. "Remarks by the President Welcoming the 2016 USA Olympic and Paralympic Teams." The White House, September 29, 2016. https://obamawhitehouse.archives.gov/the-press-office/2016/09/29/remarks-president-welcoming-2016-usa-olympic-and-paralympic-teams/.

COLIN KAEPERNICK

Associated Press. "Jaworski Praises Colin Kaepernick." ESPN, August 21, 2013. https://www.espn.com/nfl/trainingcamp13/story/_/id/9590058/ron-jaworski-says-colin-kaepernick-one-greatest-quarterbacks-ever/.

Belden, Sam. "Trump Tweeted About the NFL and National Anthem 37 Times in a Month." *Business Insider*, October 23, 2017. https://www.businessinsider.com/trump-twitter-campaign-against-anthem-protests-2017–10/.

Belson, Ken. "Fueled by Trump's Tweets, Anthem Protests Grow to a Nationwide Rebuke." *New York Times*, September 24, 2017. https://www.nytimes.com/2017/09/24/sports/trump-national-anthem-nfl.html.

Brinson, Will. "Here's How Nate Boyer Got Colin Kaepernick to Go from Sitting to Kneeling." CBS Sports, September 27, 2016. https://www.cbssports.com/nfl/news/heres-how-nate-boyer-got-colin-kaepernick-to-go-from-sitting-to-kneeling/.

Bryant, Howard. *The Heritage: Black Athletes, a Divided America, and the Politics of Patriotism*. Boston: Beacon Press, 2018.

Burton, Jamie. "'Colin in Black and White': Who Are Colin Kaepernick's Adoptive Parents Rick and Teresa?" *Newsweek*, October 30, 2021. https://www.newsweek.com/colin-black-white-who-kaepernick-adoptive-parents-netflix-1643400/.

Burton, Jamie. "Colin Kaepernick Stats: The NFL Star's College and High School Sporting Career in Numbers." *Newsweek*, November 2, 2021. https://www.newsweek.com/colin-kaepernick-high-school-college-football-statistics-1644880/.

Eligon, John, and Scott Cacciola. "As Colin Kaepernick's Gesture Spreads, a Spirit Long Dormant Is Revived." *New York Times*, September 12, 2016. https://www.nytimes.com/2016/09/13/sports/colin-kaepernick-athlete-protests.html.

Frank, Vincent. "Colin Kaepernick Situation Proves NFL Collusion Is Real and Has No Bounds." *Forbes*, November 16, 2019. https://www.forbes.com/sites/vincentfrank/2019/11/16/colin-kaepernick-situation-proves-nfl-collusion-is-real-and-has-no-bounds/.

Geragos, Mark J., Ben J. Meiselas, and Tina Glandian. "Claimant Colin Kaepernick's Demand for Arbitration." October 15, 2017. https://a.espncdn.com/pdf/2017/1015/KaepernickGrievance_r.pdf.

"Jerry Jones, Cowboys Kneel Before National Anthem Against Cardinals." NBC Sports Boston, September 25, 2017. https://www.nbcsportsboston.com/nfl/new-england-patriots/jerry-jones-cowboys-kneel-before-national-anthem-against-cardinals/369383/.

Know Your Rights Camp. https://www.knowyourrightscamp.org.

Lockhart, P. R. "Colin Kaepernick's Collusion Grievance Against the NFL, Explained." *Vox*, February 15, 2019. https://www.vox.com/identities/2018/9/6/17820158/colin-kaepernick-eric-reid-collusion-grievance-protest-settlement/.

Maske, Mark. "Colin Kaepernick Throws for NFL Scouts, Says He Has 'Been Ready for Three Years.'" *Washington Post*, November 16, 2019. https://www.washingtonpost.com/sports/2019/11/16/colin-kaepernick-workout/.

Rhodan, Maya. "This Photo of MLK Kneeling Has New Power Amid the NFL Protests. Here's the Story Behind It." *Time*, September 25, 2017. https://time.com/4955717/trump-protests-mlk-martin-luther-king-kneeling/.

Robinson, Charles. "NFL Reaches Financial Settlement with Colin Kaepernick, Eric Reid." Yahoo! Sports, February 15, 2019. https://sports.yahoo.com/sources-colin-kaepernick-withdraws-collusion-case-nfl-190149703.html.

Robinson, Charles. "6 Months Later, NFL's Colin Kaepernick Settlement Has Failed to Buy Silence." Yahoo! Sports, August 18, 2019. https://www.yahoo.com/now/6-months-later-nf-ls-colin-kaepernick-settlement-has-failed-to-buy-silence-044010622.html.

Steele, David. *It Was Always a Choice: Picking Up the Baton of Athlete Activism.* Lanham, MD: Rowman and Littlefield, 2021, 26.

Wagoner, Nick. “Transcript of Colin Kaepernick’s Comments After Preseason Finale.” ESPN, September 2, 2016. www.espn.com/blog/san-francisco-49ers/post/_/id/19126/transcript-of-colin-kaepernicks-comments-after-preseason-finale/.

Zirin, Dave. *The Kaepernick Effect: Taking a Knee, Changing the World.* New York: The New Press, 2021.

NAOMI OSAKA

Almeida, Chris. “Naomi Osaka Is Between Worlds.” *The Ringer*, December 21, 2018. https://www.theringer.com/2018/12/21/18150938/naomi-osaka-tennis-future-identity-year-in-review/.

Bergeron, Elena. “How Putting on a Mask Raised Naomi Osaka’s Voice.” *New York Times*, December 16, 2020. https://www.nytimes.com/2020/12/16/sports/tennis/naomi-osaka-protests-open.html.

Gregory, Sean. “‘This Will 100% Save Somebody’s Life.’ Athletes See a Turning Point for Mental Health After Naomi Osaka Takes a Stand at the French Open.” *Time*, June 2, 2021. https://time.com/6053239/naomi-osaka-mental-health/.

Haskell, Rob. “Leading By Example: How Naomi Osaka Became the People’s Champion.” *Vogue*, December 11, 2020. https://www.vogue.com/article/naomi-osaka-cover-january-2021/.

HuffPost Deutschland. “The Whitewashing of Naomi Osaka.” *HuffPost*, September 11, 2018. https://www.huffpost.com/archive/au/entry/the-whitewashing-of-naomi-osaka_a_23524454/.

Marine, Brooke. “Mari and Naomi Osaka Could Be the Next Venus and Serena Williams.” *W Magazine*, July 8, 2018. https://www.wmagazine.com/story/mari-and-naomi-osaka-instagram/.

McDonald, Soraya Nadia. “Naomi Osaka Made Sure Black Lives Mattered at the US Open.” Andscape, September 12, 2020. https://andscape.com/features/naomi-osaka-made-sure-black-lives-mattered-at-the-us-open/.

Meredith, Karenna. “Naomi Osaka to Skip Match After Jacob Blake Shooting: ‘Before I Am a Athlete, I Am a Black Woman.’” *Pop Sugar*, August 26, 2020. https://www.popsugar.com/fitness/naomi-osaka-jacob-blake-shooting-statement-47731526/.

“Naomi Osaka: Noodle Company Apologises for ‘White-Washing.’” BBC, January 23, 2019. https://www.bbc.co.uk/news/world-asia-46972920/.

Osaka, Naomi. “I Never Would’ve Imagined Writing This Two Years Ago.” *Esquire*, July 1, 2020. https://www.esquire.com/sports/a33022329/naomi-osaka-op-ed-george-floyd-protests/.

Rich, Motoko. "In U.S. Open Victory, Naomi Osaka Pushes Japan to Redefine Japanese." *New York Times*, September 9, 2018. https://www.nytimes.com/2018/09/09/world/asia/japan-naomi-osaka-us-open.html.

Rothenberg, Ben. "In Japan, Naomi Osaka Is an Object of Adoration and Fascination. But It's Complicated." *Slate*, January 13, 2024. https://slate.com/culture/2024/01/naomi-osaka-tennis-australian-open-japan-biography-rothenberg.html.

Thomas, Louisa. "The Thousand Autumns of Naomi Osaka." *Racquet* (blog), March 19, 2018. https://racquetmag.com/the-thousand-autumns-of-naomi-osaka/.

Victor, Daniel. "Ad Showing Naomi Osaka with Light Skin Prompts Backlash and an Apology." *New York Times*, January 22, 2019. https://www.nytimes.com/2019/01/22/world/asia/naomi-osaka-anime-ad.html.

JORDAN MARIE BRINGS THREE WHITE HORSES WHETSTONE (NÉE DANIEL)

Abdeldaiem, Alaa. "Q&A: Jordan Daniel on Raising Native American Awareness Through Running, Boston Marathon 2019." *Sports Illustrated*, April 29, 2019. https://www.si.com/edge/2019/04/29/jordan-daniel-native-american-rights-awareness-running-boston-marathon-2019/.

Adams, David Wallace. *Education for Extinction: American Indians and the Boarding School Experience, 1875–1928*. 2nd ed. Lawrence: University Press of Kansas, 2020.

Duane, Emily. "Jordan Marie Daniel Is Running for Change." Fleet Feet. Accessed July 26, 2025. https://www.fleetfeet.com/blog/jordan-marie-daniel-is-running-for-change/.

Dutch, Taylor. "How This Marathoner Is Fighting for Missing and Murdered Indigenous Women." *Runner's World*, October 28, 2020. https://www.runnersworld.com/runners-stories/a34418516/jordan-daniel-indigenous-women/.

Dutch, Taylor. "She Ran Boston with 'MMIW' Painted on Her Body for the Missing Women the World Ignored." *Runner's World*, April 25, 2019. https://www.runnersworld.com/runners-stories/a27269729/mmiw-boston-marathon-advocacy-indigenous-women/.

Estes, Nick. *Our History Is the Future: Standing Rock Versus the Dakota Access Pipeline, and the Long Tradition of Indigenous Resistance*. London: Verso, 2019.

Hogan, Wesley C. *On the Freedom Side: How Five Decades of Youth Activists Have Remixed American History*. Chapel Hill: University of North Carolina Press, 2019.

Maraniss, Andrew, and DeAndra Hodge. *Beyond the Game: Jordan Marie Brings Three White Horses Whetstone*. New York: Viking Books for Young Readers, 2025.

"Missing and Murdered Indigenous People." Office of Justice Services, Indian Affairs, US Department of the Interior. Accessed December 16, 2025. https://www.bia.gov/service/mmu/.

"Missing and Murdered Indigenous Women and Relatives (MMIWR)." National Indigenous Women's Resource Center. Accessed December 16, 2025. https://www.niwrc.org/policy-center/mmiw/.

O'Neill, Eilís. "Indigenous Runners Rosalie Fish and Jordan Marie Daniel Run for Their People." WBUR, January 3, 2020. https://www.wbur.org/onlyagame/2020/01/03/rosalie-fish-jordan-daniel-marie-mmiw/.

"On the Rise: Jordan Marie Daniel." Bandit, October 18, 2022. https://banditrunning.com/blogs/the-b-mail/on-the-rise-jordan-daniel/.

Running on Native Lands (Program). Rising Hearts. https://www.risinghearts.org/nativelands/.

"Uplift: A Conversation with Jordan Marie Daniel." International Center for Research on Women, April 28, 2021. https://www.icrw.org/uplift-a-conversation-with-jordan-marie-daniel/.

ACKNOWLEDGMENTS

So many of the athlete activists featured in this book worked hard to share the spotlight, to stop and acknowledge those who might not otherwise be seen. It seems only fitting that we follow their lead.

Several anonymous reviewers provided generous and detailed feedback that sharpened this project invaluably. It is far stronger than it would have been without their insightful contributions.

The rigor and range of this book's index is a testament to the expertise, efficiency, and generous responsiveness of Amaranth Sander at Twin Oaks, who helped power us across the finish line.

We also owe a great debt to the research assistants who contributed their energy and talent at various stages of this project. Thanks to Hope Ellis, Kylie Pascual, Mia Tenditnyy, and Emma Wickett.

And of course this book wouldn't exist without the team at the University of Illinois Press—Danny Nasset, Gary Smith, Tad Ringo, Kevin Cunningham, Jason Gabbert, Jennie Fisher, John Gehner, and all those who worked behind the scenes bringing *Athlete and Activist* to life. For their vision, skill, and tenacity throughout, we are deeply grateful.

INDEX

JULES BOYKOFF is the author of six books on the Olympics, including *NOlympians: Inside the Fight Against Capitalist Mega-Sports in Los Angeles, Tokyo, and Beyond* and *Power Games: A Political History of the Olympics.*

ALEX C. DAVIS is a writer, editor, and art director who has collaborated with media personalities, novelists, visual artists, songwriters, pastors, professors, and entrepreneurs.

AMIRA ROSE DAVIS is an assistant professor of African and African Diaspora Studies at the University of Texas in Austin and cohost of the Feminist Sports Podcast *Burn It All Down.*

MARTIN FRENCH is an illustrator, designer, and educator based in Portland, Oregon. He is the Department Chair of Illustration and a professor of illustration at the Pacific Northwest College of Art.

The University of Illinois Press
is a founding member of the
Association of University Presses.

Designed by Jason Gabbart
Composed in 11/16 Adobe Minion Pro
with League Gothic display
by Jim Proefrock
at the University of Illinois Press
Manufactured by Versa Press, Inc.

University of Illinois Press
1325 South Oak Street
Champaign, IL 61820-6903
www.press.uillinois.edu